HEROES AND SAINTS
&
OTHER PLAYS

HEROES AND SAINTS
&
OTHER PLAYS

Giving Up the Ghost,
Shadow of a Man, Heroes and Saints

Cherríe Moraga

West End Press

Selections from *Shadow of a Man* first appeared in *ZYZZYVA* and *OUTLOOK* magazines of San Francisco. An earlier version of *Shadow of a Man* was published in *Shattering the Myth: Plays by Latinas* (Arte Publico Press, 1991). *Giving Up the Ghost* was initially published in an earlier version by West End Press in 1986.

Third printing, August 2000
ISBN: 0-931122-74-0

Cover design by Nancy Woodard

Book design and typography by Prototype

Front cover painting *Calorcito de Amor* © 2000 Gabriel Navar
(www.gabrielnavar.freeservers.com)

Distributed by University of New Mexico Press

WEST END PRESS • P. O. BOX 27334 • ALBUQUERQUE, NM 87125

To my heroes,
E.G.
&
R.A.M.

CONTENTS

Giving Up the Ghost

A Stage Play in Three Portraits

If I had wings like an angel
over these prison walls
I would fly

                      (song my mother would sing me)

Giving Up the Ghost had its world premiere on February 10, 1989, at The Studio, Theatre Rhinoceros in San Francisco, with the following cast (in order of appearance):

Marisa	Belinda Ramírez
Corky	Linda Huey
Amalia	Anna Olivarez

It was directed by Anita Mattos and José Guadalupe Saucedo, with sets by Yolanda López, lights by Stephanie Johnson, and sound by Chuy Varela.

An earlier version of *Giving Up the Ghost* was produced by the Front Room Theatre in Seattle. It opened on March 27, 1987, and was directed by Laura Esparza.

The play was developed in part through the "Broadcloth Series" hosted by At the Foot of the Mountain Theatre in Minneapolis. It was given staged readings on June 16 and June 24, 1984, directed by Kim Hines.

Giving Up the Ghost was first published in book form by West End Press of Albuquerque in 1986. This current version of the play is based to a large degree on the Theatre Rhinoceros production.

CHARACTERS

MARISA, *Chicana in her late 20s*
CORKY, MARISA *as a teenager*
AMALIA, *Mexican-born, a generation older than* MARISA
THE PEOPLE, *those viewing the performance or reading the play*

SET

The stage set should be simple, with as few props as possible. A crate is used for street scenes downstage. A raised platform, stage left, serves as the bed in a variety of settings, including a hotel room, a mental hospital, and both AMALIA's *and* MARISA's *apartments. A simple wooden table and two chairs, stage right, represent* AMALIA's *kitchen. Windows, doorways, and furniture appear in the imagination when needed. The suggestion of a Mexican desert landscape is illuminated upstage during scenes evoking indigenous México. Scrims can be used for the dreamlike sequences. Aside from the minimal set pieces mentioned above, lighting and music should be the main features in providing setting. Music should be used to re-create the ''streetwise ritmo'' of the urban life of these Chicanas, spanning a generation of Motown, soul, Tex-Mex, and Latin rock. It should also reflect the profound influence of traditional Mexican folk music—rancheras, corridos, mariachi, etc.—as well as the more ancient indigenous sounds of the flauta, concha, and tambor. Throughout the long monologues (unless otherwise indicated) when the non-speaking actors remain on stage, the lighting and direction should give the impression that the characters both disappear and remain within hearing range of the speaker. In short, direction should reflect that each character knows, on an intuitive level, the minds of the other characters.*

RETRATO I
"La Pachuca"

Prologue

This is the urban Southwest, a Chicano barrio within the sprawling Los Angeles basin. Street sounds fill the air: traffic, children's schoolyard voices, street repairs, etc. MARISA sits on a wooden crate, centerstage. She wears a pair of Levi's, tennis shoes and a bright-colored shirt. Her black hair is pulled back, revealing a face of dark intensity and definite Indian features. She holds a large sketchbook on her lap. CORKY enters upstage. Their eyes meet. As MARISA's younger self, CORKY tries to act tough but displays a wide open-heartedness in her face which betrays the toughness. She dresses "Cholo style"—khaki pants with razor-sharp creases, pressed white undershirt. Her hair is cut short and slicked back. She approaches the upstage wall, spray can in hand, feigning the false bravado of her teenage male counterparts. She writes in large, Chicano graffiti-style letters, as MARISA writes in her sketchbook.

Dedicación

Don't know where this woman
and I will find each other again,
but I am grateful to her to something
that feels like a blessing

that I am, in fact, not trapped

which brings me to the question of prisons
politics
sex.

CORKY *tosses the spray can to* MARISA.

CORKY (*with* MARISA): I'm only telling you this to stay my hand.

MARISA: But why, cheezus, why me?

Why'd I hafta get into a situation where all my ghosts come to visit?
I always see that man . . . thick-skinned, dark, muscular.
He's a boulder between us.
I can't lift him and her, too . . . carrying him.

He's a ghost, always haunting her . . .
lingering.

Fade out.

Scene One

A Chicano "oldie" rises. Crossfade to CORKY *coming downstage, moving "low
and slow" to the tune.*

CORKY: the smarter I get the older I get the meaner I get
    tough a tough cookie my mom calls me
    sometimes I even pack a blade
    no one knows I never use it or nut'ing
    but can feel it there there in my pants pocket
    run the pad of my thumb over it to remind me I carry somet'ing
    am sharp secretly
    always envy those batos who get all cut up at the weddings
    getting their rented tuxes all bloody
    that red 'n' clean color
    against the white starched collars
    I love that shit!

    the best part is the chicks all climbing into the ball of the fight
    "¡Chuy, déjalo! Leave him go, Güero!" tú sabes
    you know how the chicks get all excited 'n' upset 'n' stuff
    they always pulling on the carnales 'n' getting nowhere
    'cept messed up themselves 'n' everybody looks so
    like they digging the whole t'ing tú sabes
    their dresses ripped here 'n' there . . . like a movie
    it's all like a movie

    when I was a real little kid I useta love the movies
    every Saturday you could find me there
    my eyeballs glued to the screen
    then later my friend Arturo 'n' me
    we'd make up our own movies
    one was where we'd be out in the desert
    'n' we'd capture these chicks 'n' hold 'em up for ransom
    we'd string 'em up 'n' make 'em take their clothes off
    "strip" we'd say to the wall all cool-like

funny . . . now when I think about how little I was at the time
and a girl but in my mind I was big 'n' tough 'n' a dude
in my *mind* I had all their freedom
the freedom to see a girl   kina
the way you see
an animal you know?

like imagining
they got a difernt set
of blood vessels or somet'ing like so
when you mess with 'em
it don' affect 'em the way it do you
like like they got a difernt gland system or somet'ing that
that makes their pain cells
more dense

hell I dunno

but you see
I never could
quite
pull it off

always knew I was a girl
deep down inside
no matter how I tried to pull the other off

I knew
always knew
I was an animal that kicked back . . .

(*with* MARISA) . . . cuz it hurt! (CORKY *exits.*)

MARISA (*from the platform, coming downstage*): I never wanted to be a
man, only wanted a woman to want me that bad. And they have,
you know, plenty of them, but there's always that one you can't pin
down, who's undecided. (*Beat.*) My mother was a heterosexual, I
couldn't save her. My failures follow thereafter.

AMALIA (*entering*): I am a failure.

AMALIA *is visibly "soft" in just the ways that* MARISA *appears "hard."
She chooses her clothes with an artist's eye for color and placement. They
appear to be draped over her, rather than worn: a rebozo wrapped around
her shoulders, a blouse falling over the waist of an embroidered skirt. Her
hair is long and worn down or loosely braided. As a woman nearing fifty,
she gives the impression of someone who was once a rare beauty, now
trading that for a fierce dignity in bearing.*

AMALIA: I observe the Americans. Their security. Their houses. Their dogs. Their children are happy. They are not *un* . . . happy. Sure, they have their struggles, their problemas, but . . . it's a life. I always say this, it's a life. (*She sits at the table stacked with art books, puts on a pair of wire-rim glasses, leafs through a book.*)

MARISA: My friend Marta bought her mother a house. I admire her. Even after the family talked bad about her like that for leaving home with a gabacha, she went back cash in hand and bought her mother a casita kina on the outskirts of town. Ten grand was all it took, that's nothing here, but it did save her mother from the poverty her dead father left behind. I envy her. For the first time wished my father'd die so I could do my mother that kind of rescue routine.

I wanna talk about betrayal, about a battle I will never win and never stop fighting. The dick beats me every time. I know I'm not supposed to be sayin' this cuz it's like confession, like still cryin' your sins to a priest you long ago stopped believing was god or god's sit-in, but still confessing what you'd hoped had been forgiven in you. . . . . (*Looking to* AMALIA.) That prison . . . that passion to beat men at their own game.

AMALIA: I worry about La Pachuca. That's my nickname for her. I have trouble calling her by her Christian name. (*Savoring it.*) Marisa. (*"Rain sticks" in the background.*) I worry about La Pachuca. I worry what will happen to the beautiful corn she is growing if it continues to rain so hard and much.

CORKY (*entering*): one time Tury 'n' me stripped for real
there was this minister 'n' his family down the street
they was presbyterians or methodists or somet'ing
you know one of those gringo religions
'n' they had a bunch a kids
the oldest was named Lisa or somet'ing lightweight like that
'n' the littlest was about three or so, named Chrissy
I mean you couldn't really complain about Chrissy
cuz she wasn't old enough yet to be a pain in the cola
but you knew that was coming

Lisa'd be hassling me 'n' my sister Patsy all the time
telling us how we wernt really christians
cuz cath-lics worshipped the virgin mary or somet'ing
I dint let this worry me though cuz we was being tole at school
how being cath-lic was the one true numero uno church 'n' all
so I jus' let myself be real cool with her
'n' the rest of her little pagan baby brothers 'n' sisters

that's all they was to me as far as I was concerned
they dint even have no mass
jus' some paddy preaching up there with a dark suit on
very weird
not a damn candle for miles
dint seem to me that there was any god happening in that place at all

so one day Tury comes up with this idea how we should strip
"for real"
I wasn't that hot on the idea but still go along with him
checkin' out the neighborhood looking for prey
then we run into Chrissy 'n' Tury 'n' me eye each other
the trouble is I'm still not completely sold on the idea
pero ni modo cuz I already hear comin' outta my mouth
real syrupy-like
"come heeeeere Chrissy, we got somet'ing to shooooow you"
well, a'course she comes cuz I was a big kid 'n' all
'n' we take her into this shed

I have her hand 'n' Tury tells her . . .
no I tole her this
I tell her we think she's got somet'ing wrong with her
"down there"
I think . . . I think I said she had a cut or somet'ing
'n' Tury 'n' me had to check it out
so I pull her little shorts down 'n' then her chones
'n' then jus' as I catch a glimpse of her little fuchi fachi . . .
it was so tender-looking all pink 'n' real sweet like a bun
then stupid Tury like a menso goes 'n' sticks his dirty finger on it
like it was burning hot

'n' jus' at that moment . . . I see this little Chrissy-kid
look up at me like . . . like I was her mom or somet'ing
like tú sabes she has this little kid's frown on her face
the chubby skin on her forehead all rumpled up
like . . . like she knew somet'ing was wrong with what we was doing
'n' was looking to me to reassure her
that everyt'ing was cool 'n' regular 'n' all
what a jerk I felt like!
(She pushes "Tury" away, bends down to "Chrissy".)

so, I pull up her shorts 'n' whisper to her
"no no you're fine really there's nut'ing wrong with you
but don' tell nobody we looked
we don' want nobody to worry about you"
what else was I supposed to say? ¡Tonta!
'n' Tury 'n' me make a beeline into the alley 'n' outta there!
(She exits.)

Scene Two

Crossfade to AMALIA *rising from the bed. It is morning.*

AMALIA: I remember the first time I met her, the day she first began to bring me her work. It was early morning, too early really, and there was someone at the door. At first I think it is my son, Che. Like him to appear at my doorstep with the least amount of warning. (*She goes to the "window," looks down to the front steps.* MARISA *appears, carrying a portfolio.*) But it was Marisa, standing there with a red jacket on, I remember, a beautiful color of red. Maybe if I had not dreamed the color the night before I might not even have bothered to open the door so early, such a hermit I am. (*To* MARISA:) ¿Sí?

MARISA: Hello. I got these . . . paintings. I . . . heard you could help me.

AMALIA: ¿Quién eres?

MARISA: Marisa. Marisa Moreno.

AMALIA: It's a little early ¿qué no?

MARISA: I'm sorry. Frank Delgado—

AMALIA: Súbete.

AMALIA *"buzzes"* MARISA *in.* AMALIA *puts on a robe, brushes back her hair.* MARISA *enters.*

MARISA: Good morning.

AMALIA: It's too early to tell.

MARISA: I'm sorry.

AMALIA: That's two "sorrys" already and I don't even got my eyes on yet.

MARISA: Sor . . .

AMALIA (*smiling*): Pásale. Pásale.

MARISA (*handing her a small paper sack*): Here, this is for you.

AMALIA: Siéntate.

MARISA: It's pandulce.

AMALIA (*looking inside*): Conchas. They're my favorites.

> AMALIA *puts the pastry on the table.* MARISA *sits down, holds the portfolio awkwardly in her lap. During the following scene there are brief lapses in the conversation.*

AMALIA: ¿Quieres café?

MARISA: Gracias. No.

AMALIA: Pues, yo . . . sí. (*Goes to prepare the coffee.*) I can't even talk before I have a cup of coffee in me. Help yourself to the pandulce.

MARISA (*indicating the books on the table*): Are all these yours?

AMALIA: The books? Claro.

MARISA: They're wonderful.

AMALIA: Take a look at them if you want.

> MARISA *carefully props up her portfolio onto a chair and begins to leaf through one of the books.* AMALIA *reenters, looking for her glasses.*

MARISA: You got a lotta . . . things.

AMALIA: What? Yes. Too much. My son, Che, he calls me a . . . rat pack.

MARISA: A pack rat.

AMALIA: Whatever you call it, I can't even find my glasses.

MARISA (*pointing to the painting on the upstage wall*): And this?

AMALIA: Well, I couldn't afford a room with a view, so . . . bueno, pues I improvised a little. ¿Te gusta? (*She finds her glasses in her robe pocket, puts them on.*)

MARISA: Yeah. Mucho.

AMALIA (*observing her*): You don't seem quite as awesome as Delgado described you.

MARISA: He told you about me?

AMALIA: Ay, all los boys at El Centro were talking about you, telling me how I should see your work . . . this new "Eastlos import."

MARISA: I didn't think they liked me.

AMALIA: Pues, I didn't say they *liked* you.

MARISA: Oh.

AMALIA: I think you scared them a little. Una pintora bien chingona, me dijo Frank.

MARISA: That's what he said?

AMALIA: Más o menos. Bueno. . . . *(Indicating the portfolio.)* Abrélo. Let's see what makes those machos shake in their botas so much.

As MARISA *opens the portfolio, the lights crossfade to* CORKY *entering.*

CORKY: the weird thing was that after that episode with Chrissy
     I was like a maniac all summer
     snotty Lisa kept harassing me about the virgin mary 'n' all
     'n' jus' in general being a pain in the coolie
     things began to break down with her 'n' her minister's family
     when me 'n' Patsy stopped going to their church meetings
     on wednesday nights
     we'd only go cuz they had cookies 'n' treats after all the bible stuff
     'n' sometimes had arts 'n' crafts where you got to paint
     little clay statues of blond jesus in a robe
     'n' the little children coming to him
     the drag was that you also had to do these prayer sessions
     where everybody'd stand in a circle squeezing hands
     'n' each kid'd say a little prayer
     you know like "for the starving people in china"
     Patsy 'n' me always passed when we got squeezed
     jus' shaked our heads no
     cuz it was against our religion to pray with them
     well, one time, this Lisa punk has the nerve to pray that Patsy 'n' me
     would *(mimicking)* "come to the light of the one true Christian faith"
     shi-it can you get to that? 'course we never went again

AMALIA *puts on an apron, becomes* CORKY's *"mother."*

CORKY: but I remember coming home 'n' telling my mom . . .

"MOTHER": It's better mi'jitas, I think, if you don' go no more.

CORKY: 'n' it was so nice to hear her voice so warm
　　　　like she loved us a lot
　　　　'n' that night being cath-lic felt like my mom
　　　　real warm 'n' dark 'n' kind

　　　　Fade out.

Scene Three

At rise, MARISA *straddles the kitchen chair, addresses* THE PEOPLE. AMALIA
is upstage by the bed. During MARISA's *monologue,* AMALIA *ties her hair
back into a tight bun, applies a grey powder to her face, and draws dark circles
under her eyes.*

MARISA: The women I have loved the most have always loved the man
　　　　more than me, even in their hatred of him. I'm queer I am. Sí,
　　　　soy jota because I have never been crazy about a man. (*Pause.*)
　　　　My friend Sally the hooker told me the day she decided to stop
　　　　tricking was when once, by accident, a john made her come. That
　　　　was strictly forbidden. She'd forgotten to resist, to keep business
　　　　business. It was very unprofessional . . . and dangerous. No, I've
　　　　never been in love with a man and I never understood women who
　　　　were, although I've certainly been around to pick up the pieces.
　　　　My sister was in love with my brother.

CORKY (*entering*): My mother loved her father.

MARISA: My first woman—

CORKY: The man who put her away.

MARISA: The crazy house. Camarillo, Califas. Sixteen years old.

　　　　Blue light. Haunting music. AMALIA *becomes* "NORMA," MARISA's
　　　　"*first woman.*" *She sits on the bed in a kind of psychotic stupor.* CORKY
　　　　goes over to her. MARISA *narrates.*

MARISA: When I come to get my cousin Norma, she has eyes like sau-
　　　　cers, spinning black and glass. I can see through them, my face, my
　　　　name. She says . . .

"NORMA": I am Buddha.

CORKY: How'd you get that black eye? ¿Quién te pegó?

"NORMA": I am Buddha.

Fade out.

Scene Four

CORKY *is alone on stage. She takes out a yo-yo, tries a few tricks. She is quite good.*

CORKY: since that prayer meeting night
    when Patsy 'n' me wouldn't get squeezed into the minister's jesus
    Lisa's nose was gettin' higher 'n' higher in the air

    one day Patsy 'n' her are playing dolls up
    on the second story porch of Mrs. Rodríguez's house
    it was nice up there cuz Mrs. R would let you move the tables
    'n' chairs 'n' stuff around to play "pertend"

    my sister had jus' gotten this nice doll for her birthday
    with this great curly hair
    Lisa only had this kina stupid doll
    with plastic painted-on hair 'n' only one leg
    she'd always put long dresses on it to disguise the missing leg
    but we all knew it was gone

    anyway, one day this brat Lisa throws my sister's new doll
    into this mud puddle right down from Mrs. R's porch (*She lets
    out the yo-yo. It dangles helplessly.*)

Patsy comes back into our yard crying like crazy
    her doll's all muddy 'n' the hair has turned bone straight
    I mean like an arrow!
    I wanted to kill that punk Lisa!
    so me 'n' Patsy go over to Lisa's house
    where we find the little creep all pleased with herself
    I mean not even feeling bad
    suddenly I see her bike which is really a trike
    but it's huge . . . I mean hu-u-uge!
    to this day, I never seen a trike that big
    it useta bug me to no end that she wasn't even *trying*
    to learn to ride a two-wheeler
    so all of a sudden . . . (*Winding up with the yo-yo like a pitcher.*)
    that trike 'n' Lisa's wimpiness come together in my mind
    'n' I got that thing (*Throwing the pitch.*)
    'n' I threw the sucker into the street

    I dint even wreck it none (*She stuffs the yo-yo in her back pocket.*)

but it was the principle of the thing

a'course she goes 'n' tells her mom on me
'n' this lady who by my mind don' even seem like a mom
she dint wear no makeup 'n' was real skinny 'n' tall
'n' wore her hair in some kina dumb bun
she has the nerve to call my mom 'n' tell her what I done

AMALIA, *as* CORKY's *"mom," appears upstage in an apron. She is stirring a pot in her arms. She observes* CORKY.

CORKY: so a'course my mom calls me on the carpet
    wants to know the story
    'n' I tell her 'bout the doll 'n' Patsy 'n' the principle of the thing
    'n' Patsy's telling the same story 'n' I can see in my mom's eyes
    she don' believe I did nut'ing so bad but she tells me . . .

"MOTHER": We got to keep some peace in the neighborhood, hija.

CORKY: cuz we was already getting pedo from the paddy neighbors
    'bout how my mom hollered too much at her kids . . . her own kids!
    I mean if you can't yell at your own kids who *can* you yell at?
    but she don' let on that this is the real reason
    I hafta go over to the minister's house and apologize
    she jus' kina turns back to the stove 'n' keeps on
    with what she was doing

"MOTHER": Andale, mija, dinner's almost ready. (CORKY *hesitates.*)
    Andale. Andale.

CORKY (*coming downstage*): so, a'course I go . . .
    I go by myself
    with no one to watch me to see if I really do it
    but my mom knows I will cuz she tole me to
    'n' I ring the doorbell 'n' Mrs. Minister answers
    'n' as I begin to talk that little wimp Lisa runs up
    'n' peeks out at me from behind her mother's skirt
    with the ugliest most snottiest shit-eating grin
    I'd ever seen in a person
    while all the while *I* say *I'm* sorry
    'n' as the door shuts in front of my face
    I vow I'll never make that mistake again . . .

(*with* MARISA) I'll never show nobody how mad I can get!

Black out.

Scene Five

MARISA *is pacing about* AMALIA's *room.* AMALIA *sits on the floor mixing paints. She wears a paint-splattered apron.*

MARISA (*to* THE PEOPLE): I have a very long memory. I try to warn people that when I get hurt, I don't forget it. I use it against them. I blame women for everything. My mistakes. Missed opportunities. My grief. I usually leave just when I wanna lay a woman flat. When I feel that vengeance rise up in me, I split. I desert.

AMALIA: Desert. Desierto. For some reason, I could always picture mi cholita in the desert, amid the mesquite y nopal. Always when I closed my eyes to search for her, it was in the Mexican desert that I found her. I *had* intended to take her . . . to México. She would never have gone alone, sin gente allá.

MARISA: This *is* México! What are you talking about? It was those gringos that put up those fences between us!

AMALIA *brings* MARISA *to the table, takes out a piece of charcoal from her apron, puts it into* MARISA's *hand.* MARISA *begins to sketch.*

AMALIA: She was hardly convincing. Her nostalgia for the land she had never seen was everywhere. In her face, her drawings, her love of the hottest sand by the sea.

Coming around behind her, AMALIA *wraps her arms around* MARISA's *neck. Indigenous flutes and drums can be heard in the background.*

AMALIA: Desierto de Sonora. Tierra de tu memoria. (*Turning* MARISA's *face to her.*) Same chata face. Yaqui. (*They hesitate, then kiss their first kiss.*)

MARISA: I've just never believed a woman capable of loving a man was capable of loving . . . me. Some part of me remains amazed that I'm not the only lesbian in the world and that I can always manage to find someone to love me. (*Pause.*) But I am never satisfied because there are always those women left alone . . . and unloved.

Lights slowly fade to black. Musical interlude.

RETRATO II
"La Loca"

Scene Six

A sunny morning. AMALIA is kneeling on a chair, bent over the table, painting in thick strokes and occasionally sipping at a cup of coffee. Her hair is combed into a braid and tied up. MARISA lies on the bed, hands behind her head.

AMALIA: I've only been crazy over one man in my life. Alejandro was nothing special. Era pescador, indio. Once we took a drive out of the small town he lived in, and he was terrified, like a baby. I'm driving through the mountains and he's squirming in his seat, "Amalia, ¿pa' dónde vamos? Are you sure you know where we're going?" I was so amused to see this big macho break out into a cold sweat just from going no more than twenty miles from his home town. Pero ¡Ay, Dios! How I loved that man! I still ask myself what I saw in him, really. (*Pause.*) He was one of the cleanest people I had ever met. Took two, three baths a day. You have to, you know. That part of la costa is like steam baths some seasons. I remember how he'd even put powder in his shorts and under his huevos to keep dry. He was that clean. I always loved knowing that when I touched him I would find him like a saint. Pure, somehow . . . that no matter where he had been or who he had been with, he would always have washed himself for me. He always smelled . . . so clean. (*She wipes her hands, sits at the foot of the bed.*) When I went back home that first time, after my son was already grown, I had never dreamed of falling in love. Too many damn men under the bridge. I can see them all floating down the river like so many sacks of potatoes. "Making love," they call it, was like having sex with children. They rub your chi-chis a little, then they stick it in you. Nada más. It's all over in a few minutes. ¡Un río de cuerpos muertos!

MARISA: Sometimes I only see the other river on your face. I see it

running behind your eyes. Remember the time we woke up together and your eye was a bowl of blood? I thought the river had
broken open inside you.

AMALIA: I was crazy about Alejandro. But what I loved was not so
much him . . . I loved his children. I loved the way he had made
México my home again. (*Pause.*) He was not a strong man really.
He was soft. An inside softness, I could feel even as his desire
swelled into a rock hardness. Once he said that with me he felt as
though he were "a heart that knew no sex." No man-woman, he
meant, only heat and a heart and that even a man could be entered
in this way. (*Indigenous music rises in the background.*) I, on the other
hand, was *not* clean, forgot sometimes to wash. Not when I was
around others, pero con mí misma, I became like the animals.
Uncombed. El olor del suelo.

MARISA: I remember the story you told me about the village children,
how they had put una muñeca at the door of your casita. How you
had found it there . . . there, in your likeness and you thought—

AMALIA: I must be mad.

*Suddenly, the beat of tambores. CORKY enters, wearing a native bruja
mask. She dances across the stage with rattles in her hand. As she exits,
MARISA goes to AMALIA, unbraids her hair.*

MARISA: So we take each other in doses. I learn to swallow my desire,
work my fear slowly through the strands of your hair.

*MARISA bends to kiss AMALIA on the neck. AMALIA pulls away,
comes downstage.*

AMALIA: Of course, soon after, Alejandro ran to every whore he could
find, but not without first calling me that: "puta, bruja." He claimed
I was trying to work some kind of mala suerte on him, that I was
trying to take from him his manhood, make him something less
than a man. (*Pause, to MARISA:*) I have always felt like an outsider.

MARISA starts toward her, then changes her mind and exits.

AMALIA (*to THE PEOPLE*): Ni de aquí, ni de allá. Ask me in one word
to describe to you the source of all my loneliness and I will tell you,
"México." Not that I would have been any happier staying there.
How *could* I have stayed there, been some man's wife . . . after so
many years in this country, so many years on my own? (*Pause.*) I'll
never forget the trip, the day our whole tribe left para el norte.

Sudden spiritedness. A Mexican mariachi instrumental rises. AMALIA
ties a bandana around her head. She is a young girl.

AMALIA: All of us packed into the old blue Chevy. I was thirteen and
la regla had started, the bleeding, and I was ashamed to tell my
mother. Tía Fita had been the one to warn me that at my age, any
day, I could expect to become sick. "Mala," she said, and that when
it happened I should come to her and she would bless me and tell
me how to protect myself. It came the morning of our long jornada
to California.

AMALIA *sees the "blood" coming down her leg. She takes the bandana
from her head, looks around nervously, then stuffs it under her skirt, flat-
tening it back into place.*

AMALIA: Tía Fita was not speaking to my mother so angry was she for
all of us leaving. We had asked her to come with us. "What business do I have up there with all those pochos y gringos?" My father
said she had no sense. It broke her heart to see us go. So, there was
no running to Tía Fita that morning. It seemed too selfish to tell her
my troubles when *I* was the one leaving *her.*

Southwestern desert and distant highway sounds can be heard. AMALIA,
*trying to hide from the others, pulls the bandana out from under her skirt.
Kneeling by the "river," she secretly begins to wash the blood from it.
Sound and lights gradually fade out.*

Scene Seven

MARISA *sits at the table in soft light sipping at a beer. She is dressed for the
evening in a man's suit jacket. She wears a kind of classic androgynous look.*
AMALIA *enters in a slip, crosses to the bed where she begins to dress.*

MARISA: If I were a man, things would've been a lot simpler between
us, except . . . she never would've wanted me. I mean, she would've
seen me more and all, fit me more conveniently into her life, but
she never would've, tú sabes . . . wanted me.

AMALIA: Sometimes I think, with me, that she only wanted to feel herself so much a woman that she would no longer be hungry for one.
Pero, siempre tiene hambre. Siempre tiene pena.

MARISA: She'd come to me sometimes I swear like heat on wheels. I'd
open the door and find her there, wet from the outta nowhere June
rains, and, without her even opening her mouth, I knew what she

had come for. I never knew when to expect her this way, just like the rains. Never ever when I wanted it, asked for it, begged for it, only when she decided.

AMALIA: I always had to have a few traguitos and then things would cloud between us a little and I could feel her as if underwater, my hands swimming towards her in the darkness, discovering breasts, not mine . . . not these empty baldes, pero senos firmes, like small stones of heat. Y como un recién nacido, I drink and drink and drink y no me traga la tierra.

Lights suggest memory. Nighttime freeway sounds, car radio music. MARISA and AMALIA hold each other's eyes. Voice over.

MARISA: I'll keep driving if you promise not to stop touching me.

AMALIA: You want me to stop touching you?

MARISA: No, if you promise *not* to stop.

AMALIA crosses in front of MARISA. She prepares herself a drink. MARISA watches her.

MARISA: It's odd being queer. It's not that you don't want a man, you just don't want a man in a man. You want a man in a woman. The woman part goes without saying. That's what you always learn to want first. Maybe the first time you see your dad touch your mom in that way . . .

CORKY (*entering*): ¡Hiiiijo! I remember the first time I got hip to that! My mom standing at the stove making chile colorado and flippin' tortillas. She asks my dad . . .

AMALIA (*as "MOM," to* MARISA): ¿Quieres otra, viejo?

CORKY: Kina like she's sorta hassled 'n' being poquita fría, tú sabes, but she's really digging my dad to no end. 'N' jus' as she comes over to him, kina tossing the tort onto the plate, he slides his hand, real suave-like, up the inside of her thigh. Cheezus! I coulda died! I musta been only about nine or so, but I got that tingling, tú sabes, that now I know what it means.

As CORKY exits, she throws her chin out to MARISA "bato style." MARISA, amused, returns the gesture. The lights shift. MARISA puts on a tape. A Mexican ballad is played—"Adios Paloma" by Chavela Vargas. AMALIA hums softly along with it.

MARISA: Hay un hombre en esta mujer. Lo he sentido. La miro, coci-
nando para nosotras. Pienso . . . ¿cómo puede haber un hombre
en una persona, tan feminina? Su pelo, sus movimientos de una
serenidad imposible de describir.

AMALIA (*softly singing*):

'Ya se va tu paloma, mi vida
lleva en sus alas dolor
lleva en sus ojos tristeza
y es un lamento su voz.'

MARISA (*going to her*): Tu voz que me acaricia con cada palabra . . . tan
suave . . . tan rica. (*Takes her by the hand.*) Vente.

*The music rises. They dance for a few moments, then MARISA takes
AMALIA to the bed. The music fades as MARISA slowly removes AMA-
LIA's blouse.*

MARISA: Con ella, me siento como un joven lleno de deseo. I move on
top of her. She wants this. The worn denim and metal buttons are
cotton and cool ice on my skin. And she is full of slips and lace and
stockings . . .

AMALIA: Quítate los pantalones.

MARISA: And yet it is she who's taking me.

*A soft jazz rises. MARISA takes off her jacket. They kiss each other, at first
tenderly, then passionately. They hold and caress each other. MARISA
takes AMALIA's hand, brings it to her chest. The music softens.*

MARISA: I held the moment. Prayed that if I looked long and hard
enough at your hand full inside me, if I could keep this pictured
forever in my mind . . . how beneath that moon blasting through
the window, . . . how everything was changing at that moment in
both of us.

AMALIA: How everything was changing . . . in both of us.

The jazz rises again. The lights slowly fade as they hold a deep kiss.

RETRATO III
"La Salvadora"

Scene Eight

CORKY *writes graffiti-style on upstage wall.*

>I have this rock in my hand
>it is my memory
>the weight is solid
>in my palm   it cannot fly away
>
>because I still remember
>that woman
>not my savior, but an angel
>with wings
>that did once lift me
>to another
>self.

MARISA *and* AMALIA *appear in shadow on opposite ends of the stage.*

AMALIA: You have the rest of your life to forgive me.

MARISA: Forgive you for what?

AMALIA: Por lo que soy.

Black out.

Scene Nine

AMALIA *enters carrying a small suitcase. She sets it down at the foot of the bed, removes her rebozo and holds it in her lap.*

AMALIA: All I was concerned about was getting my health back together. It was not so much that I had been sick, only I lacked . . .
energy. My body felt like a rag, squeezed dry of any feeling. Possibly it was the "change" coming on. But the women in my family did not go through the change so young. I wasn't even fifty.
I thought . . . maybe it was the American influence that causes
the blood to be sucked dry from you so early. Nothing was wrong
with me, really. My bones ached. I needed rest. Nothing México
couldn't cure.

She lies down, covers herself with the rebozo. MARISA *enters, barefoot.*

MARISA: For the whole summer, I watched the people fly in bright-
colored sails over the Califas sea, waiting for her. Red- and gold-
and blue-striped wings blazing the sky. Lifting off the sandy cliffs,
dangling gringo legs. Always imagined myself up there in their
place, flying for real. Never ever coming back down to earth, just
leaving my body behind. (*Pause.*) One morning I awoke to find a
bird dead on the beach. I knew it wasn't a rock because it was light
enough to roll with the tide . . . I saw this from a distance. Later
that day, they found a woman dead there at the very same spot, I
swear. Una viejita. (*A soft grey light washes over* AMALIA.) A crowd
gathered 'round her as a young man in a blue swimsuit tried to
spoon the sand from her throat with his finger. Putting his breath
to her was too late. She was so very very grey and wet, como la
arena . . . y una mexicana, I could tell by her house dress. How did
she drown? Then I remembered what Amalia had told me about
bad omens. (*A sudden ominous tambor,* AMALIA *bolts up in bed.*) I
stopped going. I stopped waiting.

MARISA *exits.*

AMALIA: When I learned of Alejandro's death, I died too. I just started
bleeding and the blood wouldn't stop, not until his ghost had passed
through me or was born in me. I don't know which. That Mexican
morning I had awakened to find the hotel sheets red with blood.
It had come out in torrents and thick clots that looked like a fetus.
But I was not pregnant, my tubes had been tied for years. Yet,
lying there in the cool dampness of my own blood, I felt my wom-
anhood leave me. And it was Alejandro being born in me. Does
this make sense? I can't say exactly how I knew this, except . . .
again . . . for the smell, the unmistakable smell of the man, as if we
had just made love. And coming from my mouth was *his* voice . . .
"¡Ay mi Marisa! ¡Te deseo! ¡Te deseo!" (*Her eyes search for* MARISA.)
Marisa!

Lights rise. Morning in Mexico City. AMALIA gets up from the bed.

AMALIA: It is barely dawn and the sun has already entered my hotel window. Afuera los hombres are already at work tearing up the Mexican earth with their steel claws. (*Indigenous music.*) Pero La Tierra is not as passive as they think. "Regresaré," Ella nos recuerda. "Regresaré," nos promete. When they "discovered" El Templo Mayor beneath the walls of this city, they had not realized that it was She who discovered them. Nothing remains buried forever. Not even memory. Especially not memory.

Fade out.

Scene Ten

The indigenous music blends into Chicano urban sounds. MARISA enters. Her posture is noticeably more guarded than in the previous scene. The music fades. There is a pause as MARISA scans the faces of THE PEOPLE.

MARISA: Got raped once. When I was a kid. Taken me a long to say that was exactly what happened, but that was exactly what happened. Makes you more aware than ever that you are one hunerd percent female, just in case you had any doubts. One hunerd percent female whether you act it . . . or like it . . . or not. Y'see, I never ever really let myself think about it, the possibility of rape, even after it happened. Not like other girls, I didn't walk down the street like there were men lurking everywhere, every corner, to devour me. Yeah, the street was a war zone, but for different reasons, . . . for muggers, mexicanos sucking their damn lips at you, gringo stupidity, drunks like old garbage sacks thrown around the street, and the rape of other women and the people I loved. They weren't safe and I worried each time they left the house . . . but never, never me. I guess I never wanted to believe I was raped. If someone took me that bad, I wouldn't really want to think I was took, you follow me? But the truth is . . .

CORKY (*entering*): I was took

MARISA *crosses to the platform.* CORKY *"stakes out the territory."*

CORKY: I was about twelve years old
I was still going to cath-lic school then
'n' we wore those stupid checkered jumpers
they looked purty shitty on the seventh 'n' eighth grade girls
cuz here we was getting chi-chis 'n' all

'n' still trying to shove 'em into the tops of these play suits
I wasn't too big pero the big girls looked terrible!

anyway in the seventh grade I was trying to mend my ways
so would hang after school 'n' try to be helpful 'n' all to the nuns
I guess cuz my cousin Norma got straight A's
'n' was taking me into her bed by then
so I figured . . . that was the way to go
she'd get really pissed when I fucked up in school
threatened to "take it away" tú sabes if I dint behave
can you get to that? ¡Qué fría! ¿no?

anyway Norma was the only one I ever tole
about the janitor doing it to me
'n' then she took it away for good
I'd still like to whip her butt for that
her 'n' her goddamn hubby 'n' kids now   shi-it
puros gabachos, little blond-haired blue-eyed things
the oldest is a little joto if you ask me
sure he's barely four years old but you can already tell
the way he goes around primping all over the place
pleases me to no end
what goes around comes around
"Jason" they call him
no, not "Ha-són" pero "Jay-sun"
puro gringo

anyway so I was walking by Sister Mary Dominic's classroom
"the Hawk" we called her cuz she had a nose 'n' attitude like one
when this man a mexicano motions to me to come on inside
"Ven p'aca," he says
I dint recognize him but the parish was always hiring
mexicanos to work around the grounds 'n' stuff
I guess cuz they dint need to know English
'n' the priests dint need to pay 'em much
they'd do it "por Dios" tú sabes
so he asks me, "Señorita, ¿hablas español?" muy polite y todo
'n' I answer, "Sí poquito," which I always say to strangers
cuz I dunno how much they're gonna expect outta me
"Ven p'aca," he says otra vez
'n' I do outta respect for my primo Enrique
cuz he looks a lot like him but somet'ing was funny
his Spanish I couldn't quite make it out cuz he mumbled alot
which made me feel kina bad about myself tú sabes
that I was Mexican too but couldn't understand him that good

he's trying to fix this drawer that's loose in the Hawk's desk
I knew already about the drawer

cuz she was always bitchin' 'n' moanin'
about it getting stuck cuz the bottom kept falling out
so he tells me he needs someone to hold the bottom of the drawer up
so he can screw the sides in
(*She goes to the "desk," demonstrates.*)
so standing to the side I lean over
and hold the drawer in place así
then he says all frustrated-like, "No, así, así."
it turns out he wants me to stand in front of the drawer
with my hands holding each side up así
(*She stands with her legs apart, her pelvis pressed up*
against the edge of the "desk.")
'n' believe it or not this cabrón sits behind me on the floor
'n' reaches his arm up between my legs
that I'm straining to keep closed
even though he keeps saying all business-like
"Abrete más por favor las piernas. Abretelas un poco más."
'n' like a pendeja I do

(*She grips the edge of the "desk."*)
I feel my face getting hotter
'n' I can kina feel him jiggling the drawer
pressed up against me down there
I'm staring straight ahead don' wanna look at what's happening
then worry how someone would see us like this
this guy's arm up between my legs
'n' then it begins to kina brush past the inside of my thigh
I can feel the hair   that first
then the heat of his skin
(*Almost tenderly.*) the skin is so soft I hafta admit
young kina like a girl's like Norma's shoulder
I try to think about Norma 'n' her shoulders
to kina pass the time hoping to hurry things along
while he keeps saying, "Casi termino. Casi termino."
'n' I keep saying back, "Señor me tengo que ir, mi mamá me espera."
still all polite como mensa!
until finally I feel the screwdriver by my leg like ice
then suddenly the tip of it   it feels like to me
is against the cotton of my chones

"Don't move," he tells me. In English. His accent gone. 'n' I don'

from then on all I see in my mind's eye . . .
were my eyes shut?
is this screwdriver he's got in his sweaty palm
yellow glass handle
shiny metal

the kind my father useta use to fix things around the house
remembered how I'd help him how he'd take me on his jobs with him
'n' I kept getting him confused in mind
this man 'n' his arm with my father
kept imagining he was my father returned come back
the arm was so soft but this other thing . . .
hielo   hielo   ice!
I wanted to cry, "¡Papi! ¡Papi!"
'n' then I started crying for real
cuz I knew I musta done somet'ing real wrong
to get myself in this mess

I figure he's gonna shove the damn thing up me
he's trying to get my chones down, "Por favor señor please don'."
but I can hear my voice through my own ears
not from the inside out but the other way around
'n' I know I'm not fighting this one
I know I don' even sound convinced
"¿Dónde 'stás, papi? ¿Dónde 'stás?"
'n' finally I hear the man answering, "Aquí estoy. Soy tu papá."
'n' this gives me permission to go 'head to not hafta fight

by the time he gets my chones down to my knees
I suddenly feel like I'm floating in the air
my thing kina attached to no body
flapping in the wind like a bird a wounded bird
I'm relieved when I hear the metal drop to the floor
only worry *who will see me doing this?*
(*Gritting her teeth.*) *get-this-over-with-get-this-over-with*
'n' he does gracias a dios bringing me down to earth

linoleum floor   cold
the smell of wax
polish

y ya 'stoy lista for what long ago waited for me
there is no surprise
'n' I open my legs wide wide open
for the angry animal that springs outta the opening in his pants
'n' all I wanna do is have it over so I can go back to being myself
'n' a kid again

then he hit me with it
into what was supposed to be a hole
(*Tenderly.*) that I remembered had to be
cuz Norma had found it once wet 'n' forbidden
'n' showed me too how wide 'n' deep like a cueva hers got
when she wanted it to only with me she said

MARISA: Only with you, Corky.

CORKY: but with this one there was no hole he had to make it
'n' I saw myself down there like a face with no opening
a face with no features
no eyes no nose no mouth
only little lines where they shoulda been
so I dint cry
I never cried as he shoved the thing
into what was supposed to be a mouth
with no teeth
with no hate
with no voice
only a hole
a hole!

He made me a hole!

MARISA *approaches, wraps a rebozo around* CORKY'*s shoulders, holds
her.*

MARISA: I don't regret it. I don't regret nuthin'. He only convinced me
of my own name. From an early age you learn to live with it, being
a woman. I just got a head start over some. And then, years later,
after I got to be with some other men, I admired how their things
had no opening . . . only a tiny tiny pinhole dot to pee from, to
come from. I thought . . . how lucky they were, that they could
release all that stuff, all that pent-up shit from the day, through a
hole that *nobody* could get into.

Scene Eleven

MARISA *and* CORKY *remain on stage. The lighting slowly shifts. Indigenous
music, lively tambores.* AMALIA *enters wearing a rebozo. She covers* MARISA'*s
shoulders with one as well. All three, now in rebozos, have become indias. They
enter a dream.* CORKY *comes downstage, kneels. She begins making tortillas,
slapping her hands together.* MARISA *and* AMALIA *join her on each side,
forming a half circle. They, too, clap tortillas to the rhythm of the tambores. They
are very happy. The rhythm quickens, accelerates.*

MARISA *and* AMALIA *slowly bend toward each other, their faces crossing in
front of* CORKY'*s. They kiss. Suddenly the scene darkens, the drumming becomes
sinister, the clapping frantic. Thunder. Lightning. The gods have been angered.
The three scatter. The stage is a maze of colliding lights, searching out the wom-
en.* CORKY *has disappeared.* AMALIA *cowers beneath her rebozo.* MARISA
appears upstage in shadow. She is out of breath. She is being hunted, her arms

spread, her body pressed up against an invisible wall.

MARISA: Amalia, let me in! ¡Abre la puerta! ¡Vienen a agarrarme!

    AMALIA *wrestles in bed with her "pesadilla."*

MARISA: ¡No me dejes, Amalia! ¡No me dejes sola! Let me in!

    AMALIA *can't bear to hear her, covers her ears.*

MARISA: Amalia! . . . Amalia! . . . Let . . . me . . . in!

    The lights fade out and rise again. CORKY can be seen in shadow stand-ing where MARISA had been seconds before. She holds a beer bottle in the air above her head. She comes down with it, like a weapon. The sound of glass breaking. Black out.

AMALIA (*in the darkness*): ¿Quién es? ¿Quién es? Who is it? ¿Eres tú, Che?

    Lights rise. AMALIA is sitting up in bed. There is an opened, unpacked suitcase on the floor and a photo of a man with a candle next to it on the table. MARISA appears in the doorway. She is very drunk, almost in a stupor.

AMALIA: Marisa.

MARISA: Where the . . . where have you been? (AMALIA *gets out of bed, puts on a robe.*)

AMALIA: What are you doing here?

MARISA (*menacingly*): I'm asking you a question.

AMALIA: Don't come near me.

MARISA: I said, where have you been?

AMALIA: What do you want?

MARISA: I wanna know . . . (*She stalks* AMALIA.) I wanna know where you been.

AMALIA: You're drunk.

MARISA: Good observation, maestra. Now are you gonna answer me?

AMALIA: Stay away from me. Don't touch me.

MARISA: I'm not gonna touch you. No, no. These hands? No, no, Doña Amalia . . . us jotas learn to keep our hands to ourselves.

AMALIA: ¡Adió!

MARISA: Answer me!

AMALIA: You know where I was.

MARISA: I waited for you. I waited three goddamn months! Count them! June, July—

AMALIA: I can count.

MARISA: Well, jus' cuz it aint all hanging out on the outside don' mean I don' feel nuthin'. What did you expect from me anyway?

AMALIA: Well, not this.

MARISA: Well, honey, this is what you got. Aint I a purty picture?

AMALIA: Estás borracha. Estás loca.

MARISA: Bueno, 'stoy loca. Tal vez quieres que te hable en español, eh? A lo mejor you could understand me then. I'm sorry, y'know, us pochas don' speak it as purty as you do.

AMALIA: What are you talking about?

MARISA: I'm talking about going to the goddamn mailbox every day, thinking every llamadita would be you. "Ven, Chatita. Meet me in México." You lied to me.

AMALIA: I didn't lie.

MARISA: No?

AMALIA: No. (*She turns away.*)

MARISA: What then?

There is a pause.

MARISA: Look at you. You don' got nuthin' to say to me. You don' feel a thing.

AMALIA: It's three o'clock in the morning, what am I supposed to feel?

MARISA (*after a beat*): Nuthin'. You're supposed to feel nuthin'.

AMALIA: I'm going to get you some coffee.

MARISA: I don' want no coffee! You went back to him, didn't you?

AMALIA: Ay, Marisa, por favor no empieces.

MARISA (*seeing the photo*): What is this? A little altar we have for the man? (*She picks it up.*)

AMALIA: Don't.

MARISA: ¡Vela y todo! What is he, a saint now?

AMALIA: ¡Déjalo!

MARISA: You're still in love with him, aren't you?

AMALIA: Put it down, te digo.

MARISA (*approaching*): I'm asking you a question.

AMALIA: Stay away from me.

MARISA: Answer me! (*Grabs AMALIA.*) Are you in love with him or not?

AMALIA: ¡Déjame!

MARISA (*shaking her*): Did you sleep with him?

AMALIA: No! Stop it!

MARISA: Did you? Tell me the truth!

AMALIA: No! ¡Déjame! (*They struggle. The picture falls to the floor. AMALIA breaks MARISA's hold.*) I'm not an animal! What gives you the right to come in here like this? Do you think you're the only person in the world who's ever been left waiting?

MARISA: What was I supposed to think . . . that you were dead? That you were dead or you were with him, those were my two choices.

AMALIA (*bitterly*): He's the one who's dead.

MARISA (*after a pause*): What?

AMALIA: He's dead.

> AMALIA *slowly walks over to the picture, picks it up, replaces it by the candle. She sits down on the bed, her face impassive.*

AMALIA (*after a pause*): When I got the news, I was in a hotel in Mexico City. I didn't stop to think about it, I took a bus right away to la Costa. Then I hired a boy to give me a lift in a truck. When I got to the river, I knew where to go. The exact spot. The place under the tamarindo where we used to make love. And for hours until dark I sat there by la orilla as I imagined he had that last time.

MARISA: He drowned.

AMALIA: He drowned himself.

MARISA (*going to her*): It's not your fault, Amalia.

AMALIA (*after a pause*): Whose face do you think he saw in the belly of that river moments before it swallowed him?

MARISA: It's not your fault. (*There is a long silence. MARISA makes a gesture to touch AMALIA, but is unable to.*) I shouldn't have come. I'm sorry.

AMALIA: No, stay. Stay and keep an old woman company.

MARISA: I'll come back tomorrow . . . fix the window. (*She starts to exit.*)

AMALIA: Soñé contigo.

MARISA: You did?

AMALIA: Last night. (*Pause.*) I dreamed we were indias. In our village, some terrible taboo had been broken. There was thunder and lightning. I am crouched down in terror, unable to move when I realize it is *you* who have gone against the code of our people. But I was not afraid of being punished. I did not fear that los dioses would enact their wrath against el pueblo for the breaking of the taboo. It was merely that the taboo *could* be broken. And if this law nearly transcribed in blood could go, then what else? What *was* there to hold to? What immutable truths were left? (*Pause. She turns to*

MARISA.) I never wanted you the way I wanted a man. With a man, I just would have left him. Punto. (*Pause.*) Like I left Alejandro.

The lights slowly fade to black.

Scene Twelve

MARISA *sits on the platform.* AMALIA's *rebozo has been left there.*

MARISA: I must admit I wanted to save her. That's probably the whole truth of the story. And the problem is . . . sometimes I actually believed I could, and *sometimes* she did too.

She was like no woman I had ever had. I think it was in the quality of her skin. Some people, you know, their skin is like a covering. They're supposed to be showing you something when the clothes fall into a heap around your four ankles, but nothing is lost, y'know what I mean? They jus' don' give up nuthin'. Pero Amalia . . . ¡Híjole!

She picks up AMALIA's *rebozo, fingers it.*

She was never ever fully naked in front of me, always had to keep some piece of clothing on, a shirt or something always wrapped up around her throat, her arms all outta it and flying. What she did reveal, though, each item of clothing removed was a gift, I swear, a small offering, a suggestion of all that could be lost and found in our making love together. It was like she was saying to me, "I'll lay down my underslip. ¿Y tú? ¿Qué me vas a dar?" And I'd give her the palm of my hand to warm the spot she had just exposed. Everything was a risk. Everything took time. Was slow and deliberate.

I'll never forget after the first time we made love, I was feeling muy orgullosa y todo, like a good lover, and she says to me—

AMALIA (*voice-over, memory*): You make love to me like worship.

MARISA: And I nearly died, it was so powerful what she was saying. And I wanted to answer, "Sí, la mujer es mi religión." If only sex coulda saved us.

Y'know, sometimes when me and her were in the middle of it, making love, I'd look up at her face, kinda grey from being indoors so much with all those books of hers, and I'd see it change, turn this real deep color of brown and olive, like she was cooking inside. Tan linda. Kind. Very very very kind to me, to herself, to the pinche planet . . . and I'd watch it move from outside the house where that crazy espíritu of hers had been out makin' tracks. I'd watch it come inside, through the door, watch it travel all through her own private miseries and settle itself, finally, right there in the room with us. This bed. This fucking dreary season. This cement city. With us. With me. No part of her begging to have it over . . . forget. And I could feel all the parts of her move into operation. Waiting. Held. Suspended. Praying for me to put my tongue to her and I knew and she knew we would find her . . . como fuego. And just as I pressed my mouth to her, I'd think . . . *I could save your life.*

(*Coming downstage.*) It's not often you get to see people this way in all their pus and glory and still love them. It makes you feel so good, like your hands are weapons of war. And as they move up into el corazón de esta mujer, you are making her body remember, it didn't have to be that hurt. ¿Me entiendes? It was not natural or right that she got beat down so damn hard, and that all those crimes had nothing to do with the girl she once was two, three, four decades ago.

Pause. Music rises softly in the background.

MARISA: It's like making familia from scratch
each time all over again . . .
with strangers, if I must.
If I must, I will.

I am preparing myself for the worst
so I cling to her in my heart
my daydream with pencil in my mouth

when I put my fingers
to my own forgotten places.

The lights gradually fade out. Music.

End

Shadow of a Man

It was said that these were enough
to keep mindful of what was in shadow
and what was dawning.

Popul Vuh

Family is the place where
for better or worse
we first learn to love.

Loving in the War Years

Shadow of a Man had its world premiere in San Francisco on November 10, 1990, produced by Brava! For Women in the Arts and the Eureka Theatre Company. It was directed by María Irene Fornes, who also designed the set. It included the following cast (in order of appearance):

Lupe	Jade Power
Rosario	Jennifer L. Proctor
Hortensia	Alma Martínez
Leticia	Raquel Haro
Manuel	Carlos Barón
Conrado	Luis Saguar

The costumes were designed by Gail Russell, lighting by Tim Wessling, and the stage manager was Christi-Anne Emerson. Special thanks to Ellen Gavin, artistic director of Brava! For Women in the Arts, who initially sought out *Shadow of a Man* and saw it to full production.

Shadow of a Man was a recipient of the Fund for New American Plays Award and received major support from the Rockefeller Foundation. The play was originally developed through INTAR's 1985 Hispanic Playwrights-in-Residence Laboratory in New York City under the direction of María Irene Fornes. *Shadow of a Man* was presented as a staged reading from February 23–26, 1989, at the tenth Los Angeles Theatre Center's New Works Festival. José Luis Valenzuela directed. It was then produced as a "play in progress," directed by Joy Carlin, at the American Conservatory Theatre's Playroom from April 20–28, 1989. On August 12, 1989, a later version was presented as a staged reading at the South Coast Repertory's Hispanic Playwrights' Festival. It was directed by Amy Gónzales.

The published text is primarily based on the Brava–Eureka production, with some revisions made subsequently by the playwright.

CHARACTERS

LUPE, *the younger daughter, 12*
ROSARIO, *the aunt, mid-50s*
HORTENSIA, *the mother, mid-40s*
LETICIA, *the older daughter, 17*
MANUEL, *the father, early 50s*
CONRADO, *the compadre, early 50s*

(Compadre *refers to the relationship of a godfather to the parents of his godchild. In Mexican culture, it is a very special bond, akin to that of blood ties, sometimes stronger.*)

SETTING

1969. The action takes place in the home of the Rodríguez family in Los Angeles over a period of about a year.

The play opens into the interior of the house to the places chiefly inhabited by mothers and daughters. The kitchen is the central feature with the bathroom (stage right) and daughters' bedroom (stage left). Downstage is the porch, surrounded by the family garden of chiles, nopales, and roses. Props and set pieces have been kept to a minimum, only what is essential to the action. Rooms are divided by representative walls that rise about sixteen inches from the floor, yet still give the impression of providing some minimal privacy for secrets both shared and concealed. There is an exit upstage center.

The backdrop to the house is a Mexican painting of a Los Angeles sunset. As the light descends into garden, the smoggy sky takes on a faint mixture of orange and lavender, a pastel rose against the stark silhouette of cactus and palm trees; multiple plant life abounds.

ACT I

Scene One

At rise, spot on LUPE, staring with deep intensity into the bathroom mirror. She wears a Catholic school uniform. She holds a lit votive candle under her chin and a rosary with crucifix in her hand. Her face is a circle of light in the darkness. The shadow of the crucifix looms over the back wall.

LUPE: I think there's somethin' wrong with me. I have ex-ray eyes. (*Staring.*) I can see through Sister Genevieve's habit, through her thick black belt with the rosary hanging from it, through her scapular and cotton slip. She has a naked body under there. I try not to see Sister Genevieve this way, but I can't stop. (*Pause.*) I look at other kids' faces. Their eyes are smart like Frankie Pacheco or sleepy like Chela La Bembona, but they seem to be seeing things purty much as they are. Not ex-ray or nuthin'. (*Pause.*) Sometimes I think I should tell somebody about myself. It's a sin to have secrets. A'least the priest is apose to find out everything that's insida you. I try. I really do try, but no matter how many times I make confession, no matter how many times I try to tell the priest what I hold insida me, I know I'm still lying. Sinning. Keeping secrets. (*She pauses before the reflection, then blows out the candle.*)

ROSARIO *appears in the garden. She wears a bandana around her head and an apron around her thick middle. She picks a few chiles, tastes them. Moments later, LUPE enters.*

ROSARIO (*chewing on a chile*): I still say que los chiles no saben buenos aquí. I think it's the smog. They don' taste like nut'ing. Aquí en Los Angeles the sun has to fight its way down to the plantas . . . and to the peepo, too. (*Takes another bite. To LUPE:*) No sabe a nada. Try one.

LUPE: No, these things are like fire.

ROSARIO: Prúebalo, gallina.

LUPE (*taking the chile and very gingerly taking a bite off the top*): Hmm. Not so bad. (*Swallows.*) ¡Ay, tía! You tricked me. (*Fans her mouth.*)

ROSARIO: ¡Eres gringuita!

LUPE: I swear I dunno how you can eat them like they were nuthin'.

ROSARIO: Vas a ver when your tía is kicked the bucket and is gone, you'll be there in your big Hollywood mansion haciendo tortillas y el chile, nomaś to remember me. Or maybe you'll get la criada mexicana to do it.

LUPE: I won't have a maid. I don't believe in that.

ROSARIO: Es trabajo like any other work. There will always be ricos, an' the rich peepo always need someone to clean up after them. ¿Sabes qué? En México, half the woman got criadas. Allá you don' have to be rico to have one.

LUPE: That's why it's better here.

ROSARIO: ¿Por qué?

LUPE: People don't have to be maids.

ROSARIO: Bueno, pero la tierra no me da ni un chile verdadero. (ROSARIO *crosses to the rose bushes.*) Mijita, ¿me traes el agua?. Tienen tanta sed estas rosas. I don' know why I let them go so long sin agua. (LUPE *brings her the watering can.*) Gracias, mija. Make sure you cut a few of these para la mesa. Mañana es Sábado.

LUPE: Flowers won't make this Saturday any better.

ROSARIO: It's your brother's wedding.

LUPE: I'm never leaving home like Rigo.

ROSARIO: Never say never, hija. (*She continues watering.*) Ya, ya. No 'stén enojaditas conmigo. You're thirsty ¿no, mis rositas? Tomen el agua. Ya, ya . . .

LUPE: Why do you talk to them, tía?

ROSARIO: To who, las plantas?

LUPE: Yeah.

ROSARIO: Because they got souls, the same as you and me.

LUPE: You believe that?

ROSARIO: It's true.

LUPE: The nuns don't say that.

ROSARIO: And you think the nuns are always right?

LUPE: I guess so.

ROSARIO: God is always right, not the Church. The Church is made by
    men. Men make mistakes, I oughta know. (*To the roses*:) ¡Ay, pobre-
    citas! ¡Qué mala madre soy, mis pobres rositas! Tomen, tomen el
    agua. Ya, mis hijitas . . . mis rositas.

LUPE: Tía, you know how they say that . . . that when you get that chill
    that goes through your body—

ROSARIO: Es el diablo que te toca.

LUPE: Yeah, the devil. He comes up and kinda brushes past you, touch-
    ing you on the shoulder or somethin', right?

ROSARIO: Sí, pero es un dicho nomás.

LUPE: Pero ¿sabe qué, tía? A veces I do feel him. El diablo me entra a
    mí. He's like a shadow. I can barely tell he's there, jus' kinda get a
    glimpse of him outta the corner of my eye, like he's following me
    or somethin', but when I turn my head, he's gone. I jus' feel the
    brush of his tail as he goes by me.

ROSARIO: ¿Tiene cola?

LUPE: Sí.

ROSARIO: El diablo.

LUPE: I tole you and I get a chill all over.

ROSARIO: No hables así, hija. I don' know what those monjas teach you
    at tha' school sometimes.

LUPE: The nuns never tole me this.

ROSARIO: Well, take it out of your head. It's not good for you.

LUPE: It's not like I'm making myself think about it, it jus' keeps pop-
    ping up in my head. It's like the more I try not to think about some-
    thin', the more it stays in my head. I mean your mind jus' thinks
    what it wants to, doesn't it?

ROSARIO: No, you gottu train it. If you don', it could make you a very
    unhappy girl.

LUPE: I try, but I can't. At night, I try to stay awake cuz when I fall asleep
    that's when he sneaks inside me. I wake up con tanto miedo. It's
    like my whole body's on fire and I can hardly breathe. I try to call
    Lettie pero la voz no me sale. Nuthin' comes out of my mouth.

ROSARIO: You gottu stop thinking like tha'. Tu mamá y yo, we had a
    cousin, Fina, a very good-looking girl, but she thought about el

diablo y la religion y todo eso so much that she went crazy. Se volvió loca, hija.

LUPE: You think I'm going to go crazy, tía?

ROSARIO: No, mija.

LUPE: Is it a sin to think like this?

ROSARIO: No sé, mija. I don' think so. Not if you can't help it.

LUPE: Sometimes I jus' feel like my eyes are too open. It's like the more you see, the more you got to be afraid of.

ROSARIO: ¿Quieres saber la verdad, Lupita?

LUPE: What?

ROSARIO: Only los estúpidos don' know enough to be afraid. The rest of us, we learn to live con nuestros diablitos. Tanto que if those little devils wernt around, we woont even know who we were. (*Collecting the roses.*) Vente. Today we think about las rosas. Sundee, cuando we go to church, there's plenty a time to think about el diablo.

Scene Two

Crossfade to the kitchen, where a "telenovela" (a Mexican soap opera) plays on the TV. HORTENSIA, wearing a house dress and apron, is rolling out tortillas onto a chopping block. There is a kind of grace to her movements as she alternately crosses to the stove, where she heats the tortillas on the comal, then back to the board again. LUPE and ROSARIO are seated next to each other at the kitchen table, engrossed in the novela. For a few moments all that is heard are the muted voices coming from the TV and the steady beat of the rolling pin.

HORTENSIA: She can go to hell as far as I'm concern.

ROSARIO: Who, Hortensia?

HORTENSIA: La gringa. They didn't even get married yet, and she's already got my son where she wants him. Ni lo conozco. He's a stranger. (*She puts the tortilla on the comal, watches it rise.*) The other day, Rigo comes home from the college. Manuel sees him in the door, and of course he jumps up from the chair para darle un abrazo. And you know what Rigo does?

ROSARIO: What?

HORTENSIA: He pushes Manuel away.

ROSARIO: No!

HORTENSIA: And you know what he says?

ROSARIO: ¿Qué?

HORTENSIA: He says, "No, Dad. I'm a man now. We shake hands."

ROSARIO: No me digas.

HORTENSIA: Te digo. Does that sound like my son to you?

ROSARIO: No.

HORTENSIA: And to see the look on Manuel's face. . . . Y la girl standing there with a smile en la cara.

ROSARIO: ¡Que barbaridad!

HORTENSIA: It's eating Manuel up. (*She gestures that* MANUEL *has been
drinking.*)

ROSARIO: Tha's not so good, Tencha.

HORTENSIA (*intimately*): Claro que no. Pero ¿qué puedo hacer yo?

LUPE: Miren. María's telling Enrique she's pregnant.

ROSARIO: No! ¿de veras?

*They all stop and watch, mesmerized. Muffled voices emerge from the TV,
then commercial.*

LUPE: ¡Ay, wait til he finds out quien es el padre!

ROSARIO: ¡Híjole!

HORTENSIA (*resuming her work*): But, I tell you one of this days I'm
gointu tell esa gringuita everything I think of her. She thinks she
gointu keep my son, holding him all to herself? But, they're a difernt
kina peepo, los gringos, . . . gente fría. I try to tell Rigo this before
they were novios que iba tener problemas con ella pero no me quiso
escuchar. They might fool you with their pecas y ojos azules, but
the women are cold.

ROSARIO: I bet her thing down there is already frozen up.

HORTENSIA (*loving it*): ¡Ay, Rosario, no digas eso!

ROSARIO: I may be old . . . but my thing is still good 'n' hot ¿verdad,
mija? Us mexicanas keep our things muy caliente . . . as hot as tha'
comal allí ¿no?

LUPE: I dunno, tía.

ROSARIO: ¿No sabes? ¿Tú no sabes, eh? (*Snatches playfully at* LUPE *between the legs.*) Is your fuchi fachi hot down there, too?

LUPE (*jumping away*): Stop, tía!

HORTENSIA: Chayo!

ROSARIO: ¡Ay, tú eres pura gallina!

LUPE comes up behind HORTENSIA and takes a warm tortilla from the stack. HORTENSIA slaps her hand lightly.

HORTENSIA: With you around, the stack never gets any bigger.

LUPE: But my panza does. (*She sticks out her stomach.*)

ROSARIO: Now you look like María on the novela.

LUPE begins to enact "la desesperada" role as LETICIA enters. She is wearing late '60s Chicana "radical" attire: tight jeans, large looped earrings, an army jacket with a UFW (United Farm Workers) insignia on it.

HORTENSIA: Allí viene la política. (*To* LETICIA:) I tole you I don' wan' you to wear esa chaqueta.

ROSARIO: Es el estilo, Tencha.

LETICIA (*stealing a warm tortilla from the stack*): Yeah.

HORTENSIA: ¡Tú también!

LETICIA (*putting butter on the tortilla*): How can you stand watching those things? Those novelas are so phony. I mean, c'mon. What do you think the percentage of blondes is in México?

ROSARIO: No sé.

LETICIA: I mean in relation to the whole population.

ROSARIO: No sé.

LETICIA: One percent? But no, the novelas make it look like half the population is Swedish or something. Even the maids are güeras. But, of course, the son of the patrón falls madly in love with one and they live happily ever after in luxury. Give me a break!

HORTENSIA: Ni modo, I enjoy them.

ROSARIO: Es pura fantasía. Pero mija, they got so many problemas, it gets your mind off your own.

LETICIA: I guess that's the idea.

Offstage, a man's heavy, labored steps.

MANUEL: Hortensia! Hortensia!

HORTENSIA: ¡Ay, that man's gointu make me crazy! Lupita, go see what your papi wan's.

LUPE: Sí, mami.

HORTENSIA: Y si te pide cigaros, don' give him none.

LUPE: Okay. (*She exits.*)

ROSARIO: ¿Todavía 'stá fumando?

LETICIA: Like a chimney.

HORTENSIA: Sure! He wants to kill himself. He's not suppose to smoke. Es otro día que no trabaja. I don' know what we're gointu do if he keep missing work.

ROSARIO: He dint see el doctor?

LETICIA: Are you kidding?

HORTENSIA: He's scare to death of them. He complain que he pull something in his arm on the job, que le duele mucho. But I don' believe it. I think it's his heart. The other night he woke up in the middle of the night and he could har'ly breathe. He was burning up. I had to get up to change all the sheets y sus piyamas . . . they were completely soak. Now he's gottu take the sleeping pills jus' to close his eyes for a few hours. Pero vas a ver, tonight he'll go out again.

LETICIA (*kissing* HORTENSIA *on the cheek*): Pues, ay te watcho.

HORTENSIA: ¿A dónde vas?

LETICIA: To Irma's.

HORTENSIA: ¿Qué vas a hacer con ésa?

LETICIA: Oh, we're jus' gonna hang out for a while.

HORTENSIA: Well, not on the street, do you hear me?

LETICIA: Aw, Mom!

HORTENSIA: Aw, Mom!

ROSARIO: Déjala, Tencha.

HORTENSIA: Pero no la conoces, es callejera.

LETICIA: Shoot, I'll be graduating in a month.

HORTENSIA: You think graduating makes you una mujer? Eres mujer cuando te cases. Then your husband can worry about you, not me.

LETICIA: Yeah, but Rigo can come and go as he pleases whether he's married or not.

HORTENSIA: Claro. Es hombre.

LETICIA: Es hombre. Es hombre. I'm sick of hearing that. It's not fair.

HORTENSIA: Well, you better get usetu things not being fair. Whoever said the world was gointu be fair?

LETICIA: Well my world's going to be fair!

> LETICIA *exits upstage.* ROSARIO *and* HORTENSIA *stare at the air in silence.*

HORTENSIA: Te digo the girl scares me sometimes.

LUPE (*entering*): Papi wants his cigarettes.

> *A beat, then all three simultaneously turn their attention back to the novela. The lights fade to black while the novela continues playing in the darkness. It gradually fades out.*

Scene Three

Late that night. Offstage, a car pulls up, then a door slams. The sound of keys being tossed and a man's heavy steps. MANUEL *enters, drunk. He wears a hat and a light jacket. From the point of his entrance, the scene assumes a stylized, surreal quality. Characters' actions seem to slow down into almost ritualized movement. This scenario has replayed itself many times in the lives of the Rodríguez family.*

MANUEL: Rigo, mijo. I can't touch you no more. I have to tie my hands down to keep them from reaching for you. Cuz it goes against my nature, not to touch the face of my son. (*He sits, takes off his hat.*) You usetu sit and converse with me. Your eyes were so black, I forgot myself in there sometimes. I watched the little fold of indio skin above your eyes, and felt those eyes hold me to the ground. They saw. I know they saw lo que sabía mi compadre, that I am a weak man, but they did not judge me. Why do you judge me now, hijo? How does the eye turn like that so suddenly?

HORTENSIA (*entering*): ¿A quién 'stás hablando?

MANUEL (*as if snapping out of a trance*): He doesn't got a mind no more.

HORTENSIA: Who?

MANUEL: Who do you think? (*He looks at her.*) She's took his mind.

> HORTENSIA *goes to* MANUEL, *begins to undress him.*

HORTENSIA: And who's took your mind, talking to yourself como un loco?

MANUEL (*rising*): What was my son given huevos for? Tell me. For some spoiled gabachita to come along and squeeze the blood white from them?

HORTENSIA: No hables cochino. Siéntate. (MANUEL *sits; she removes his shoes.*)

MANUEL: You know what they call men like that que let the women do their thinking for 'em? Pussywhipped, that's what they call 'em.

HORTENSIA: No seas grosero. The girls are gointu hear you.

MANUEL: My son is a pussywhipped!

HORTENSIA: Estás borracho. I dunno how you gointu get up for the wedding tomorrow. (*She unbuttons his shirt.*)

MANUEL: Ni modo. I'm not going.

HORTENSIA: No empieces.

MANUEL: No voy.

HORTENSIA: Quítate la camisa.

MANUEL: We're not good enough for them, that's what they think! Y tú eres igual que Rigo. You jus' want to put on the face in front a those gringos. (*Digging at her.*) They don' even let your sister come.

HORTENSIA: They said it's gointu be a small ceremony.

MANUEL: ¡A la chingada! A small ceremony.

HORTENSIA (*unbuckling his pants*): How you think Rigo's gointu feel without his padre there?

MANUEL: He's gonna feel nothing. Rigo's got no feelings no more.

HORTENSIA: You're not gointu do this to me ¿m'oyes?

MANUEL: Where's my baby? (*He rises, hoists up his pants.*)

HORTENSIA: Manuel.

MANUEL: Quiero verla.

HORTENSIA: You're not gointu leave us solitas to go into the church tomorrow.

MANUEL: ¡Mija! ¡Mijiiita!

HORTENSIA: Leave the girls alone.

MANUEL: ¡Mija! (*He tries to fasten his pants, fumbling.*)

HORTENSIA: Why do you think your son lef' this house?

MANUEL: Because he's a gabachero!

HORTENSIA: Because you make him ashame, coming home smelling de los bars.

MANUEL: Coming home con el cheque en la mano to feed you.

HORTENSIA (*severely*): Tiene ojos. He can see what you are.

MANUEL: ¡Soy hombre! (*He takes a feeble swing at her, misses.*)

HORTENSIA: ¡Pégame! Es lo único que sabes.

A shot of pain rushes through MANUEL's *arm. He doubles over.*

HORTENSIA: Your heart, te molesta.

MANUEL: No.

HORTENSIA: Pero sigues tomando. I'm gointu get your pills. (*She starts for the bathroom.*)

MANUEL: ¡No, no necesito nada!

HORTENSIA (*with disdain*): I should let you die.

LETICIA *appears at the doorway.*

MANUEL: Y ¿qué quieres tú?

LETICIA: What did you do to her?

MANUEL: I didn't touch her.

LETICIA: Did he hit you?

MANUEL: What I say is not good enough for you, metiche?

HORTENSIA: Déjala.

MANUEL: You wanna defend your mother? You think cuz your brother's gone, que you're the macho around this house now?

LETICIA: No.

MANUEL: I'm sick of this house full of viejas.

LETICIA: Why don't you leave then?

HORTENSIA: Leticia!

MANUEL: If my compadre could see how you and Rigo turned out . . .

HORTENSIA: That's enough!

MANUEL: Eres fría ¿sabes? You're cold as a piece of ice . . . jus' like your mother.

HORTENSIA (*glaring at* MANUEL): I wish I had a heart of stone.

HORTENSIA *goes out to the porch, takes out a cigarette and lights it.* MANUEL *crosses to the girls' bedroom.* LETICIA *remains in the kitchen. Lights rise on* LUPE *in bed, the covers pulled up tight around her. She clutches a rosary in one hand.* MANUEL *stands at the doorway, his shadow filling it.*

MANUEL: I know la chiquita is waiting for me. She's got a soft heart, mi niñita. She makes sure her papacito comes home safe.

HORTENSIA: If he doesn't give a damn about himself, why should I care?

MANUEL (*going to* LUPE): Lupita! ¿'Stás durmiendo, hijita? (*He lays his huge man's head on* LUPE's *small shoulder.*) You'll never leave me ¿no, mijita?

LUPE: No, papi.

MANUEL: Eres mi preferida ¿sabes?

LUPE: Sí, papi.

MANUEL: You're different from the rest. You got a heart that was made to love. Don't ever leave me, baby.

LUPE: No, papi. I won't.

He begins to weep softly. Her thin arm mechanically caresses his broad back. A muted tension falls over the scene. A few moments later, LETICIA *enters the bedroom, brings* MANUEL *to his feet.*

LETICIA: C'mon, Dad. Let's get you to bed now.

He gets up without resistance. LETICIA *holds him up as they exit. Fade out.*

Scene Four

The next morning. LETICIA *is standing in front of the bathroom mirror fixing her hair, while* LUPE *polishes a pair of white dress shoes. They are wearing bathrobes.* MANUEL *sits on the porch, drinking a beer, a six-pack next to him. It is cloudy out. Lucha Villa's "Que me lleva el tren" is playing on the radio.*

RADIO:

'Estoy al punto de volver contigo.
Estoy al punto de subirme al tren . . .'

LUPE: I liked Teresa better.

LETICIA: I liked Teresa, too, but Rigo thought he was too good for a Chicana, so he's gonna marry a gringa.

LUPE: Well, he mus' love Karen.

LETICIA: Right.

LUPE: Doesn't he?

LETICIA (*holding a bang in place*): I can never get these bangs to lay right.

LUPE: Well, does he?

LETICIA: Does he what?

LUPE: Love her. Does he love Karen?

LETICIA: Who knows what he feels, man. Jus' forget it. Do you hear me? Don't think about him no more. He's gone. In a couple of hours he'll be married and that's it. We'll never see him again. (*Beat.*) Hand me the Dippity Do.

LUPE *gets up, gives* LETICIA *the styling gel.* LETICIA *begins applying it to her bangs.* LUPE *moves in front of* LETICIA *into the face of the mirror. She stretches open her eyelids with her fingertips.*

LETICIA: Lupe, get out the way.

LUPE: You can see yourself in there . . . in the darkest part.

LETICIA: What?

LUPE: Two little faces, one in each eye. It's like you got other people living inside you. Maybe you're not really you. Maybe they're the real you and the big you is just a dream you.

LETICIA: I swear you give me the creeps when you talk about this stuff. You're gonna make yourself nuts.

LUPE: But I'm not kidding. I mean how d'you know? How do you really know what's regular life and what's a sueño?

LETICIA: You're talking to me, aren't you? That's no dream. (*Holds her hand up to* LUPE.) How many fingers do you see?

LUPE: Five.

LETICIA: Right! (*Grabs* LUPE's *face.*) Five fingers around your fat little face. You feel this?

LUPE: Yeah. Yeah.

LETICIA: That's what's real, 'manita. What you can see, taste, and touch . . . that's real.

LUPE: I still say you can't know for sure.

LETICIA: Say something else. You're boring me.

LUPE (*putting her shoes on*): I went over to Cholo Park yesterday.

LETICIA: You better not tell Mom. Some chick jus' got her lonche down there the other day. They found her naked, man, all chopped up.

LUPE: Oooh. Shaddup.

LETICIA: Well, it's true. What were you doing down there?

LUPE: Nuthin'. Jus' hanging out with Frankie and her brother, Nacho.

LETICIA: God, I hate that huevón. Stupid cholo. He jus' hangs out with you girls cuz nobody his own age will have anything to do with him. So, what were you guys up to?

LUPE: Nuthin'.

LETICIA: C'mon. Fess up! Out with it!

LUPE: Nuthin'. The boys were jus' throwing cats.

LETICIA: What?

LUPE: They was throwing cats off the hill.

LETICIA: Whadda you mean?

LUPE: Well, they stand up there, grab the gatos by the colas and swing 'em above their heads and let 'em go. ¡Ay! They let out such a grito! It's horrible! It sounds like a baby being killed!

LETICIA: And you watch that shit?

LUPE: They was the ones doing it! Most of the time the gatos land on their feet. But this one time this one got caught on these telephone wires. It jus' hung there in shock with its lengua así. (*She sticks out her tongue dramatically.*)

LETICIA: ¡Ay! Stop it! I swear you're really sick. How can you stand to see 'em do that?

LUPE: It's hard to take your eyes off it.

LETICIA: Si-ick. (*Holding her hair in place.*) Here, Lupe. Stick the bobby pin in for me.

LUPE: Where?

LETICIA: Back here. C'mon, my arm's getting tired. (LUPE *does it.*) Ouch! ¡Bruta! You want to draw blood or what?

HORTENSIA *walks through the kitchen toward the porch. Her hair and face are done. She wears dress shoes and a house robe. She carries* MANUEL's *suit.*

HORTENSIA: I hear too much talking in there!

LUPE: We'll be right out, mami!

HORTENSIA: We're gointu be late for the wedding!

LETICIA (*muttering*): Ask me if I care.

Crossfade to HORTENSIA *at the screen door of the porch.*

HORTENSIA (*to* MANUEL): I got your clothes ready.

He ignores her, turns up the volume on the radio.

RADIO:

'Voy a tratar de ser feliz como antes
y si no puedo que me lleva el tren.'

ROSARIO *enters from the garden.*

ROSARIO: If you listen too much to that music, you start to believe there's
something good about suffering.

MANUEL: ¿Qué dices?

ROSARIO: I don' believe in suffering . . . for nobody.

MANUEL: Siéntate.

ROSARIO: You're gointu be late for la boda, Manuel.

MANUEL (*cracking open a beer for her*): Toma.

ROSARIO *sits as* HORTENSIA *turns away. They watch her exit.*

MANUEL (*lowering the volume on the radio*): Salud. (*They toast, clinking
bottles.*) One of these days, I'm gonna get in the car, buy me a coupla six-packs and hit the road and I'm not gonna stop until I reach
the desert. They got the road paved now all the way to my pueblito.
I'll stop off and see my compadre in Phoenix. Conrado's got a real
nice life there. He's getting rich, I bet, pouring cement holes in the
ground. He's making swimming pools. Everybody's got a swimming
pool out there. (*There's a slight rumbling in the sky.*)

ROSARIO: It's gointu rain.

MANUEL (*observing the sky for a moment*): In Arizona, it rains when you
least expect it. You got thunder and lightning and the whole sky
lights up. (*Thunder is heard. He takes a swig of beer.*) I remember when
I was a little esquincle, riding in the back of my tío's troque. We was
coming back from digging ditches or something, me and a buncha
primos all piled up in back, jus' watching the sky get darker and
darker. Suddenly the lightning flashed and the whole desert lit
up and you could see the mountain with the camel back clear as
noontime. Then, crack! The thunder came and it started raining
cats and dogs. In minutes the water soaked up all the dust of the
road and it smelled real clean. Then right there in the open back
of the troque, we tore off our clothes and took our showers in the
rain. (*Another swig.*) Sometimes, you know, you want to be a boy
like that again. The rain was better then, it cleaned something.

LUPE (*standing at the screen door, dressed for the wedding*): Papi?

MANUEL *turns to* LUPE. *They all freeze. The lights and music fade.*

Scene Five

Days later. Afternoon. HORTENSIA *is sorting beans at the table while* LETI-CIA *shows* ROSARIO *snapshots from Rodrigo's wedding.*

LETICIA: Mira, tía. Look at all the stiffs lined up in a row.

ROSARIO: ¡Ay, Leticia!

LETICIA: You didn't miss much, tía. All they gave you was a little drop of lousy champagne and this white cake that stuck to the roof of your mouth. (*Shows her a picture.*) Don't we look miserable?

ROSARIO: I haftu admit you look like a buncha sourpusses.

LUPE (*entering*): What bothered me was the stupid dress I had to wear.

HORTENSIA: You look purty, mija.

ROSARIO: Wasn' tha' the dress you wore for Easter?

LUPE: Yeah.

LETICIA (*taking out another photo*): Look. Karen's mother is spose to be younger than my mom and she already looks like she's ready for the grave!

HORTENSIA (*to* ROSARIO): You know how güeras' skin gets arrugas so young.

ROSARIO: It's true.

LETICIA: Well, I feel sorry for Rigo cuz his wife is gonna be a has-been in no time. It runs in their genes, you can tell.

ROSARIO: Don' you have anyt'ing nice to say about the wedding?

HORTENSIA: Rigo looked real handsome. He smelled good, too. I got to say it, I got a good-looking boy. He had on a beautiful white . . . como lino . . . suit and a kina grey tie with a tiny design in it, muy fino. I think era de seda.

LETICIA: Probably la vieja bought it for him, so he'd look classy enough for them.

HORTENSIA: Tu hermano has more class than all those peepo put together.

LETICIA: You don't have to tell me that! Tell him. He's the one trying to get over.

ROSARIO: Déjame ver otra, Lupita.

LETICIA (*sarcastically*): Oh, that's us standing by the "horn of plenty," the big banquet table.

HORTENSIA: Chayo, you could of died of starvation there. We didn't eat before cuz I thought they'd feed us at the wedding. Pero you know, the peepo that got the most are the tightest with their money.

ROSARIO: Tha's why they got it.

LETICIA: I dunno. The cacahuates they had in the little platitos really filled me up.

LUPE (*sing-songy*): Ca-ca-huates. Ca-ca-huates. I like that word!

LETICIA: You just like the "caca" part.

LUPE: Shad-dup.

> HORTENSIA *shows* ROSARIO *another photo.* LUPE *and* LETICIA *start exploring a packet of old photos.*

HORTENSIA: This is el marido. Not a bad-looking man, really. (*Almost proud.*) He's a doctor.

ROSARIO: ¿De veras?

HORTENSIA: I think for the babies.

LETICIA: A pediatrician.

ROSARIO: Uh huh. Y ¿qué pasó when they saw que Manuel wasn' with you?

HORTENSIA: When we came in, the mother—

LETICIA: She knew something was up.

HORTENSIA: I guess she could tell from our faces. I felt so ashame to walk in there without my husband, and I sure wasn't gointu tell her que he refuse to come. But she didn't give me a chance to say nothing. She jus' grab me by the arm and, right away like she har'ly notice, says to me, "Oh, I'm so sorry Mr. Rodríguez couldn't make it, I hope it's nothing serious." Pero muy suave.

LETICIA: And then she took us into this big room, introducing us to all these stiffs, going (*very upper-class WASP*), "Isn't it a pity that Mr. Road-ree-gays had to be ill today . . . of all days!" It got me ill!

ROSARIO: ¿Había mucha gente?

LETICIA: ¡Montones!

HORTENSIA: Sí. Mucha. It was a lie that there was no room for our family.

LETICIA: They were afraid that if too many Mexicans got together, we'd take over the joint. Bring out the mariachi, spill guacamole over everything . . .

HORTENSIA: They jus' didn't want us.

LUPE: You should've been there, tía.

ROSARIO (*a bit martyred*): No importa. Y Rigo dint say nut'ing tampoco about his papá?

HORTENSIA: Ni una palabra.

ROSARIO: ¡Válgame Dios!

HORTENSIA: When we came into the church, me besó en la cara. "Hello, Mother," he says to me, muy formal . . . y nada más.

ROSARIO: ¡No me digas!

HORTENSIA: Te digo . . . y la girl had nothing to say to me neither. She hug me—

LETICIA: Cold enough to freeze the dead.

LUPE (*taking out another photo*): Oooh! I like this picture of you, Lettie. What grade were you in?

MANUEL *enters unnoticed. He stands behind the women.*

LETICIA: What grade, mamá?

HORTENSIA (*examining the photo*): Kinnergarten.

LUPE: I like your little curly top. (*They pass it around, amused.*)

ROSARIO: Se parece a Chirlee Temple ¿no?

HORTENSIA (*tossing LETICIA's hair*): Un poco.

LUPE (*with another photo*): Who's this, mami? (*Passes it on to HORTENSIA.*)

HORTENSIA: Este . . . that's . . . Conrado.

LUPE: Who's that?

ROSARIO: A friend of your papi's, mija.

HORTENSIA: His compadre.

LUPE: He's really handsome. Where's he at?

HORTENSIA (*nervously*): No sé. I don' know where he is. Don' talk about him.

LUPE: Why? Is he dead or something?

HORTENSIA: No, he's not dead!

LUPE: God, I jus' asked.

HORTENSIA: Pues, no seas tan preguntona. It makes tu papi . . . (MANUEL *comes up from behind and takes the photo from HORTENSIA's hand.*) . . . nervioso.

MANUEL: I've been looking for this.

HORTENSIA (*gathering up the photos, to the girls*): Mira. You messed up all my pictures. Next time I wannu find something, I won' be able to. Put them away now. I can't pass the whole day here contando los chismes. Put all these fotos away now!

As the rest of the lights fade, a spot remains on MANUEL *staring at the picture. A look of nostalgia passes over his face as "Sombras" by Javier Solis rises. Fade out.*

'Sombras nada más, acariciando mis manos,
sombras nada más, en el temblor de mi voz . . .'

Scene Six

Many months later. A Saturday afternoon. HORTENSIA *is changing Rodrigo's baby on top of the kitchen table, making the usual exclamations a grandmother does over her first grandchild.*

HORTENSIA: ¡Ay, mi chulito! ¡Riguito! ¡Qué precioso! . . .

LETICIA (*offstage*): Mom, I got the car!

HORTENSIA: Is that you, hijas?

LUPE (*entering with* LETICIA): It's so tuff, mami!

HORTENSIA: Miren lo que tengo aquí.

LETICIA: It's jus' an old jalopy, but I can fix it up.

LUPE: Hey! When'd Sean come?

HORTENSIA: ¡Ay, don' call him that! It sounds like a girl's name.

LETICIA: That's what they called him.

HORTENSIA: Well, I call him Riguito, como su papá, not . . . Shawn!

LETICIA: Yeah, well jus' don't try calling him that in front of Karen. What's he doing here anyway?

HORTENSIA: She left me the baby to watch. Qué milagro ¿eh?

LUPE: That's for sure.

HORTENSIA: Una 'mergency came up. She tole me would I mind watching the baby. I said of course not. Even though they only call me when they need me.

LETICIA: Where's Rigo?

HORTENSIA: He has the army this weekend. ¡Ay! You should of seen how handsome he look in that uniform! He remind me of your papá.

LETICIA: The entire Raza's on the streets protesting the war and my brother's got to be strutting around in a uniform.

HORTENSIA: Es mejor que he should of gone to Vietnam?

LETICIA: No, but he doesn't have to go around parading it. God, I hope nobody I know saw him.

HORTENSIA: No te entiendo.

LUPE: Lettie got the car, Mom.

HORTENSIA: I know, mija. (*To* LETICIA:) But don' think this means you are free to go wherever you please now. Es para ir al trabajo, nomás.

LETICIA: I paid for it.

HORTENSIA: And who's paid for you for the las' eighteen years of your life?

LETICIA (*doesn't respond; she dangles her car keys over the baby; then, with a thick "chola" accent*): Hey, little guy. You wannu go cruising with me, ése?

HORTENSIA (*taking out various articles from the diaper bag*): She brought enough things for a week. And she gave me a long list of instructions. You think I dint already have three babies of my own. (*Changing the diaper, to the baby:*) ¡Fuchi! Apestas. (*The baby sprays her.*) ¡Ay, Dios! Miren. He soak me. (*Wiping herself.*) No mijito, you haftu learn not to shoot tu pajarito in the air. I forgot since I had you girls, Riguito usetu do the same thing. I'd get it right in the face sometimes.

LUPE: Ugh!

HORTENSIA: They don' know yet to control their little pipis.

LUPE: Let me have the keys, Lettie. (LETICIA *gives them to her.*)

LETICIA: He is a little cutie, but I don't know about that blond hair.

LUPE (*dangling the keys over the baby*): The rest of him is brown.

HORTENSIA: Mi güerito. He's as purty as they get to be. Miren, su pajarito es igual a de Rigo when he was a baby.

LETICIA: Please, spare me.

LUPE: Really?

HORTENSIA: Igualito. (*To the baby:*) You got your papi's thing, mi Riguito. (*To her daughters:*) Dicen que esta parte siempre es the true color del hombre, el color de su . . . nature.

LETICIA: Does that make him a real Mexican then?

HORTENSIA: Mira, qué lindo es . . . like a little jewel. Mi machito. That's one thing, you know, the men can never take from us. The birth of a son. Somos las creadoras. Without us women, they'd be nothing but a dream.

LETICIA: Well, I don't see you getting so much credit.

HORTENSIA: But the woman knows. Tú no entiendes. Wait until you have your own son.

LETICIA: Who knows? Maybe I won't have kids.

HORTENSIA: Adió. Then you should of been born a man. (*She finishes changing the baby.*)

LETICIA: I'm gonna go wash the car. You want to help, Lupe?

LUPE (*dangling the keys*): I'll be there in a second.

LETICIA: Well, give me the keys then. (LUPE *does.* LETICIA *starts to exit.*)

HORTENSIA: When you're done, you can go pick up the panza from Pedro's Place. I wannu make menudo for the morning.

LETICIA: All right. All right. (*She exits.*)

HORTENSIA: ¡Ay! They grow up so fast, Lupita. In only minutes, los muchachitos are already standing at the toilet, their legs straight like a man's. I remember sometimes being in the kitchen and hearing little Riguito, he must of been only three or so, going to the toilet by himself. The toilet seat flipped back. Bang! it would go. Then the stream from his baby's body. But the sound was like a man's, full . . . y fuerte. It gives you a kind of comfort, that sound. And I knew the time would fly so fast. In minutes, he would be a man. (*To the baby:*) You, too ¿no, mijito? You got your papi's thing. El color de la tierra. A sleeping mountain, with a little worm of life in it. Una joya. Ya ya, duérmete, mi chulito.

LUPE: Duérmete.

Fade out.

Scene Seven

LETICIA *is practicing dance steps in the kitchen to the tune of "I Heard it through the Grapevine." She sings along.* LUPE *sits on the front porch, drawing.*

LETICIA: 'Oh I heard it through the grapevine . . . And I'm just about to loooose my mind.'

MANUEL (*entering, carrying a lunch pail*): Apaga la música.

LETICIA (*turning down the radio*): You're home early.
MANUEL: Apágala. (LETICIA *turns it off, glaring at him.*) Don't look at me in the eyes like that. You look at your father con respeto ¿m'oyes?

LETICIA: I hear you.

MANUEL (*muttering as he passes*): If my compadre could see you now, it'd break his heart.

LETICIA: I don't even remember him, Dad.

> MANUEL *stops, looks at her absently, then exits.*

LETICIA (*going out onto the porch*): I bet they're gonna fire him.

LUPE: You think so, Lettie?

LETICIA: Yeah.

LUPE: He's sick.

LETICIA: He's not sick. He's drunk. (*She sits on the step.*)

LUPE (*after a pause*): I wish Rigo'd come home and take me down to the cañón like he usetu cuz everything would be better there.

LETICIA: I'll take you, . . . soon as I get the car running again.

LUPE: I never told mami pero sometimes Rigo'd leave me there by myself.

LETICIA: I bet when he took Carmen along.

LUPE: Yeah, (*Pause.*) but it was jus' fine with me. I'd pack a little lonche, una manzana, un taco de papas and fill a jar up with chocolate. Then I'd find my special spot by the stream and sit myself down to eat. (*Pause.*) Funny, being alone by that riyito makes everything different. It's like the cañón is a cathedral greater than any church you've ever seen. Más grande que even la misión and there you can really feel God in the incense, the viejitas kissing their rosaries . . . and just the oldness of the place. It echoes con las voces de los ancianos. But the cañón is different, even older . . . and God, a lot kinder. (*Pause.*) I can never put a face to Him out there. I just feel Him in a way that makes my whole body disappear. Not like I'm a ghost or somethin', but just that my body doesn't matter. I mean it doesn't matter any more than the little pajarito landing on the ramita or the tiny stream of water that cools my toes. And I feel so light, like an astronaut or somethin', weightless, with no worries holding me down to the ground.

LETICIA: You feel free there.

LUPE: Yeah, that's how it feels, Lettie. It feels free.

The lights fade to black.

Scene Eight

HORTENSIA *and* ROSARIO *are just finishing folding clothes on the kitchen table. It is a humid evening.* HORTENSIA *wears a light robe.*

HORTENSIA: For weeks now, I walk around the house and hold my breath. Conrado is the only name on Manuel's lips. He don' talk about nothing else.

ROSARIO: ¿Qué dice, Hortensia?

HORTENSIA: Estupideces. Half the time, I can't understand him. I see him sitting on the toilet, crying. I go to him, "Manuel ¿qué tienes?" Pero no responde. His heart is as closed as this. (*Makes a fist.*) I can't make him open up to me. No puedo. He miss work already two times this week. And the week before, another two days. El patrón call him this morning. He wouldn't go to the phone.

ROSARIO: You're going to make yourself sick, worrying so much about him.

HORTENSIA: How often does he have anything to do with me? Once in a blue moon. I touch his feet in bed and he freezes. No soy tan vieja. I don' wannu give up, Chayo. If I give up, I might as well put on the black dress and say I'm a dead man's wife.

ROSARIO: Then don' give up, sister. Make your husband see you. Grab his face and make him see you. It's not that men don' love. They jus' don' stop to see a woman. Us women do all the seeing for them. If a man sighs for no reason, we already know the reason. We watch their faces y sabemos cuando se vuelvan máscaras. What they hide from us, we smell on their clothes and hear en sus sueños. We know better than them what they feel . . . and tha's enough to make us believe it's love. Tha's a marriage.

HORTENSIA: Pues para mí, ya no. It's not a marriage for me.

ROSARIO (*after a pause*): Tencha, sooner or later, we choose.

HORTENSIA: ¿Qué quiere decir eso?

ROSARIO: Bueno, I know sometimes you look at me and think there's somet'ing wrong with me becuz I coont stay with a husband.

HORTENSIA: That's not true, hermana.

ROSARIO: But after you see the other side of a man, your heart changes.

It's harder to love. I've seen tha' side too many times, mija. (*Pause.*) Ahora, tengo me casita, mi jardín, my kids are grown. What more do I need?

HORTENSIA: I need more, Chayo. (*She carries the basket of clothes upstage.*) I think about Conrado sometimes . . . the way he walked into a room . . . like a warrior, un gallo. His plumas bien planchadas. His shoes shined, the crease in his pantalones sharp like swords . . . y tan perfumado, you could smell him before you saw him. I remember how when Conrado touch me . . . jus' to grab my hand nomás, and los vellitos on my arm would stand straight up. (*Pause.*) I've never felt that with Manuel.

ROSARIO: Conrado was not the kina man you marry, hija.

HORTENSIA: He never ask me.

ROSARIO: Yo sé.

MANUEL can be seen coming up the porch steps from the garden. He carries a caged canary.

ROSARIO: Allí viene.

MANUEL sets the cage on the porch, removes his jacket. He wears a sleeveless undershirt, sits and stares at the canary.

MANUEL: Lupita's lying to me. She knows. I know she knows. She puts her little hand on my back and pats me real softly. "It's okay, papi," she says. "It's okay." But I know she's just waiting for the day she can get away from me.

ROSARIO: Me voy, hermana. Nos vemos mañana.

HORTENSIA: 'Stá bien. Buenas noches.

They embrace. ROSARIO exits upstage. MANUEL enters, still mumbling to himself. He doesn't notice HORTENSIA until she speaks.

HORTENSIA: Manuel. (*He stops.*) Touch me. (*Pause.*) Yo existo. (*Pause.*) Manuel, yo existo. Existo yo. (*He walks past her.*) Nothing's changed, has it? I look at your back and it tells me nothing's changed. A back doesn't cry, ni tiene sonrisa, ni sabe gemir, gritar. But this is what I look at day in and day out.

He doesn't move. She approaches him.

HORTENSIA (*tenderly*): You know how good I know this back? (*Lightly touching him, he stiffens.*) I know it mejor que tú. ¿Sabes que tienes a scar right here? (*Touching it.*) ¿Y un lunar allí? (*Touching.*) ¿Y otro acá? (*Pounding his back.*) ¡Mirame, cabrón! Why don't you look at me? ¡Mirame!

MANUEL (*spinning around, grabbing her by the wrists*): No, you take a good look at me!

HORTENSIA: Manuel!

MANUEL: Everywhere I go, everybody's laughing at me. The girls, they're laughing at me all the time. The people I work with, the patrón . . . he's laughing, too. Nobody knows our secret, but they all know and they're all laughing at what they see inside my head.

HORTENSIA: ¡No es cierto!

MANUEL: You don' think I hear you laughing every day at the big joke? (*Pushes her away violently.*)

HORTENSIA: No!

MANUEL: I don' need this! I got friends. I don' need to suffer no more on account a you!

HORTENSIA (*going to him*): ¡Manuel, por favor!

He slaps her, throws her to the floor, then pulls her up by the hair.

MANUEL: You make me sick ¿sabes? I can't stand for you to touch me!

He drops her to the floor, grabs his jacket and the bird and exits. HORTENSIA sobs, starts crawling on the floor to the bathroom. Her face is bruised. LUPE enters.

LUPE (*running to her*): Mami, ¿qué pasó? Did papi hurt you, mami?

HORTENSIA: Estoy sucia.

LUPE: No, mami.

HORTENSIA: Me tengo que bañar. (*Looks up at LUPE with glazed eyes.*) Oh, eres tú, hija. Vente, mi bebita. I haftu give you a bath.

LUPE: What, mami? I don't need a bath.

HORTENSIA (*pulling at LUPE's clothes*): I haftu take off your piyamita and your little diaper.

LUPE: No, mami.

HORTENSIA: I'll put you in the water.

LUPE: ¿Qué 'stás diciendo, mamá?

HORTENSIA (*trying to drag LUPE to the bathroom*): Don' worry. I'm gointu test the water first con el dedito. (*Pulls her.*)

LUPE: Stop, mami. You're hurting me.

HORTENSIA (*catching the fear in LUPE's eyes*): Don' look at me like that! (*Covering LUPE's eyes.*) ¡No puedo soportarlo! (LUPE *begins to cry.*)

Conrado. . . . You got his eyes. Why you gottu have his eyes?

HORTENSIA buries LUPE's face into her lap, holds LUPE down, covering her face and mouth. LUPE struggles, cries out.

HORTENSIA: I have to turn off the sound. No llores más, bebita. (*Smothering LUPE's cries, she pushes her head onto the floor.*) I cover your little head with my hand and push it down into the water. (*LUPE stiffens.*) Your piernitas stop kicking. Your skin turns white and your little hands float up like a toy baby. Sí. Eso. Everything is quiet.

LUPE passes out. She lies limp on the floor. There is a pause, then HORTENSIA suddenly realizes what she has done.

HORTENSIA: ¡Dios mío! ¿Qué he hecho? I killed her. ¿Para qué? For him? ¿Qué he hecho? ¿Qué he hecho?

LUPE stirs, sits up. HORTENSIA, hysterical, rushes to the bathroom. She grabs a douche bag and a bottle of vinegar. LETICIA enters. LUPE runs to her.

LUPE: Lettie, it's mami.

HORTENSIA climbs into the tub, starts to pour the vinegar into the bag, her hands shaking. LUPE stands back, horrified. LETICIA goes to HORTENSIA.

LETICIA: Mamá, what are you doing?

HORTENSIA: ¡Estoy cochina! Filthy!

LETICIA: Did he hit you, mamá?

HORTENSIA: ¡Me tengo que lavar! ¡Me voy a bañar! (*She abandons the bag, pouring vinegar directly all over herself. LETICIA tries to get the bottle from her.*)

LETICIA: No, mamá. ¡Dámela!

HORTENSIA: ¡Déjame sola! ¡'Stoy sucia! ¡Desgraciada!

LETICIA: Mamá, you're gonna hurt yourself, let it go!

HORTENSIA: Tu padre thinks I stink, pues now I stink for sure!

LETICIA: Give me it! (*She grabs the bottle. HORTENSIA slumps into the tub, holding her bruised face.*)

HORTENSIA: ¿Por qué no me mata tu papá? ¿Por qué no? It'd be better if he kill me!

LUPE (*softly*): No llores, mami.

LETICIA: Let me see your eye.

HORTENSIA: No me toques. 'Stoy sucia.

LETICIA (*putting a washcloth to the bruise*): C'mon, mamá. Now, hold it there. (*Removes* HORTENSIA's *robe.*) God, you're drenched in the stuff.

HORTENSIA (*seeing* LUPE, *to* LETICIA): ¡Díle que se vaya! I don' want her to see me!

LETICIA: Lupe, go get another bata. (LUPE *doesn't move.*)

HORTENSIA: ¡No quiero que me vea!

LETICIA: Now! (LUPE *runs out.*)

HORTENSIA: I'm sorry you gottu see me así, mija.

LETICIA (*drying* HORTENSIA's *shoulders*): It's okay, mamá. It's not your fault.

HORTENSIA: I guess all my girls are grown up now.

LETICIA: Yeah.

> LETICIA *unties* HORTENSIA's *hair.* LUPE *enters with the robe.* LETICIA *puts it over* HORTENSIA's *shoulders, dries her hair.*

HORTENSIA: ¿Sabes que, Leticia? Tu hermanita es una señorita now.

LUPE: ¡Ay, mami!

LETICIA: I know, mamá.

HORTENSIA (*to* LUPE): No, ya no eres baby. You gottu behave a little difernt now, mija. Tú sabes, . . . con más vergüenza. You can't go jumping around all over the place con los chavos like before.

LUPE (*soberly*): Sí, mami.

HORTENSIA: I got no more babies. (*To* LUPE:) Vente.

> LUPE *goes to her. They embrace.* LUPE *massages* HORTENSIA's *shoulders.* LETICIA *sits on the edge of the tub, watching.*

HORTENSIA: You got good hands, hija. Now, I'm your baby ¿no, mija? Now you have to clean my nalguitas jus' like I wipe yours when you was a baby.

LUPE: ¡Ay, mami!

HORTENSIA: You girls are all I got in the world, you know.

LUPE: Sí, mami. Sí.

> *"Sombras" rises as the lights gradually fade to black.*

> 'Sombras nada más, entre tu vida y mi vida.
> Sombras nada más, entre tu amor y mi amor.'

ACT II

Scene One

Sunset. A few months have passed. ROSARIO *sits on the porch. She fans herself.* LUPE *sits on the step below her.* LETICIA *lies on top of the bed. "Evil Ways" by Santana plays in the background.*

'Oh you got to change your evil ways, baby . . .' (*The music gradually fades.*)

LUPE: Papi keeps talking to himself all the time. Maybe he's a saint.

ROSARIO: Tu papá no es un santo, mija.

LUPE: He could be. He suffers inside like the saints.

ROSARIO: Alotta peepo suffer. It doesn' make them saints.

LUPE: Maybe he'll die and it'll be our sin because we didn't know he was a saint.

ROSARIO: Don' say that. Some peepo suffer because they wannu.

LUPE: I don't wannu.

ROSARIO: So don'. But your papi wan's to suffer.

LUPE: He doesn't. He has something inside . . . that hurts him.

ROSARIO: What?

LUPE: I dunno.

LETICIA (*from the bedroom*): Lupe!

LUPE: What?

LETICIA: Are you gonna do my toenails?

LUPE: Yeah!

MANUEL *enters the kitchen from upstage center, talking silently to himself. An orange color washes over the scene.* ROSARIO *looks to the horizon.*

ROSARIO: Mira. Ya se pone el sol. (*They all observe the sunset for a moment.*) This is the bes' time of the day. ¿Ves las sombras?

LUPE: They're so clear.

ROSARIO: En esta hora, jus' before the sun sets, you see the shadows more clear than any time of the day.

The sunset colors deepen, then fade as the sun descends into the horizon. LUPE *goes to the kitchen, pulls a chair out for her father to sit.* ROSARIO *exits upstage.* LUPE *sits at* MANUEL's *feet, rubs some dirt off his shoe.* MANUEL *takes out the photo of Conrado from the breast pocket of his shirt. He stares at it, then puts it on the table.*

MANUEL: When my compadre Conrado was a little boy, he usetu shine shoes for a living. He was never ashamed of it because, like he said, it was about making a buck any way you could. He built the little shoeshine box with his own hands. I watched him do it. He sawed six perfeckly even rectangles of wood and hammered them together. He made the top piece so it could flip open and shut. Like this. (*He demonstrates.*) And then he sanded it con una piedra. He painted the box black because most of the shoes he shined were black, he said, and that way the box would never look dirty. But the Tucson streets were very dusty in those days and the polvo would seep into the cracks of the box anyway. (*Pause.*) You don't know him, Lupita. But my compadre is an American success story. He usetu live here . . . near us. But then he went back to Arizona to make it big.

LETICIA: Lupe!

LUPE: Yeah! . . . I'm coming! (*She starts to go.*)

MANUEL: Lupita. (LUPE *stops.* MANUEL *stares at her absently.*)

LUPE: ¿Sí, papi?

MANUEL *walks out mumbling to himself. He has left the photo on the table.* LUPE *picks it up, studies it.*

LETICIA: Lupe!

LUPE: Okay!

She stuffs the photo into her pocket and crosses to the bedroom. LETICIA *hands her a bottle of nail polish.* LUPE *sits by the foot of the bed and starts applying polish to* LETICIA's *toes.* LETICIA *keeps reading.*

LUPE: What name did you choose for your confirmation, Lettie?

LETICIA: Cecilia.

LUPE: Why Cecilia? Saint Cecilia was burned at the stake.

LETICIA: I liked the name.

LUPE: I was thinking of Magdalena for me. . . . Naw, cuz then people call you Maggie. That's Maggie O'Connell's name. I can't stand her.

LETICIA: They could call you Lena. Anyway, nobody calls anybody by their confirmation name. It's just on paper.

LUPE: Yeah, but I love the story about her.

LETICIA: Who?

LUPE: Mary Magdalene. (*She rises, begins to dramatize the story.*) I love how she jus' walked right through all those phony baloney pharisees, right up to the face of Jesus. And there they were all looking down their noses at her like she was nuthin' but a . . . tú sabes, a fallen woman.

LETICIA: Well, she was a prostitute.

LUPE: She doesn't look to the right or to the left, jus' keeps staring straight ahead. The pharisees try to stop her, but Jesus tells them, "Let her come forward." (*Returns to the toes.*)

LETICIA: Make sure you get it all the way down to the cuticle.

LUPE: I am. (*She paints one toe, then goes back to her story.*) So the crowd opens up and makes a path for her. And then she kneels down in front of Jesus and jus' starts crying and crying for all the sins she's done. (*Sobs dramatically at the feet of "Jesus."*) And y'see his feet are dusty from all those long walks in the desert. She's crying up a storm. It's coming down in buckets all over Jesus' feet. (*Sob, sob, sob.*)

LETICIA: Are you finished?

LUPE: In a minute. But suddenly the tears become like bath water, real soft and warm and soothing-like. She's got this hair, y'see, this long beautiful dark hair and it's so thick she can make a towel out of it. It's so soft, it's almost like velvet as she spreads it all over Jesus' feet. (*She pours her hair over "Jesus' " feet, then returns to* LETICIA's *toes.*)

LETICIA: Blow on 'em a little, will you? So they can dry faster. (LUPE *does.*)

LUPE: Can you imagine what it musta felt like to have this woman with such beautiful hair *wiping* it on you? It's jus' too much to think about. And then Jesus says . . . (*She grabs* LETICIA's *hand as if* LETICIA *were Mary Magdalene.*) "Rise woman and go and sin no more." Now that's what I call forgiveness. That's . . . relief.

HORTENSIA (*offstage*): Lupita! Lupe!

ROSARIO (*offstage*): Lupe! ¡Tu mamá te 'stá llamando!

LUPE: God, I'm everybody's slave around here.

> LUPE *exits. "Evil Ways" rises in the background. The light and the music gradually fade out.*

Scene Two

MANUEL *is talking to the caged canary in the garden. He drinks from a bottle of tequila. It is dusk.*

MANUEL: I am a lonely man. I bring the bottle to my lips and feel the tequila pour down behind my tongue, remojando the back of my throat. Corre down la espina, until it hits my belly and burns como madre in there. For a minute, I am filled up, contento . . . satisfecho. (*Pause.*) I look across the table and my compadre's there y me siento bien. All I gotta do is sit in my own skin in that chair. (*Pause.*) But he was leaving. I could smell it coming. I tried to make him stay. How did I let myself disappear like that? I became nothing, a ghost. I asked him, "Do you want her, compa?" And he said, "Yes." So, I told him, "What's mine is yours, compadre. Take her." (*Pause.*) I floated into the room with him. In my mind, I was him. And then, I was her too. In my mind, I imagined their pleasure, and I turned into nothing.

Black out.

Scene Three

MANUEL, LETICIA *and* LUPE *are seated at the kitchen table.* LUPE *wears a Catholic school uniform.* HORTENSIA *is making breakfast.* LUPE *and* LETICIA *are eating.* LETICIA *puts the food to her mouth without lifting her eyes from the college textbook she is reading.* MANUEL *is writing a letter.*

HORTENSIA: Leticia, if you read while you eat, the food doesn't set right in your stomach.

LETICIA: I'm all right.

LUPE: You got a test, Lettie?

LETICIA: A mid-term.

LUPE: Is college hard?

LETICIA: Uh-huh.

HORTENSIA: Don't bother your sister, hija. Tiene que estudiar.

LUPE: I wanna go to college, too.

LETICIA: You should try to get a scholarship. Go to Harvard or something.

LUPE: What's Harvard?

LETICIA: The best.

HORTENSIA puts a plate of food down for MANUEL. He ignores it.

HORTENSIA: What are you doing?

MANUEL: Writing a letter.

HORTENSIA: You're not gointu eat?

He doesn't respond. They all look at him. After a beat, LUPE takes a slip of paper and a pen from her book bag, goes to HORTENSIA.

LUPE: Mami, I need my confirmation form signed.

HORTENSIA: Dásela a tu padre.

LUPE: Will you sign this for me, papi? (*MANUEL ignores her. LUPE points to the signature line.*) Right here. (*He continues writing the letter. HORTENSIA signs the form.*) Thanks, mami.

LETICIA: You ready, Lupe?

LUPE: Yeah.

They gather their things to leave, kiss their mother, then their father. MANUEL does not respond.

LETICIA: See ya, Dad.

LUPE: Bye, papi.

LETICIA (*exiting*): 'Bout the time you're in college, lots of Chicanos will be going to Harvard. You'll see.

LUPE: Where's it at?

LETICIA: Cambridge, Massachusetts.

LUPE: Too far.

LETICIA (*calling out*): I'll be home late! Gotta work tonight!

HORTENSIA: Okay, mija!

LUPE: Bye, mami!

HORTENSIA: ¡Qué les vaya bien!

HORTENSIA clears off the table. MANUEL is addressing an envelope. She brings him a cup of coffee. He pushes it away very slowly the full length of his arm.

HORTENSIA (*after a pause*): Why are you writing him?

MANUEL: Because he's my compadre.

HORTENSIA: Y ¿quién soy yo?

MANUEL: You're my wife.

HORTENSIA: Sí, soy tu esposa. Cuando tienes hambre, I put the food in front of you. When you're sick, I force the medicine into your mouth. I iron your pantalones and put out clean piyamas for you each night. Every time you take a bath, I wash out the ring in the tub.

MANUEL *tears the page from the writing tablet.* HORTENSIA *takes an envelope from her apron and tosses it onto the table.*

HORTENSIA: You asked him to come back.

MANUEL (*grabbing the envelope*): You read this? . . . You read my compadre's letter?

HORTENSIA: Sí, la leí.

MANUEL: You had no right. Do you see your name on this sobre?

HORTENSIA: No.

MANUEL: Pues, until my compadre puts your name here, you got no right to read what he writes to me.

HORTENSIA: Why, Manuel? Why you want that man back in our lives?

MANUEL: No te importa a tí. My compadre's coming back cuz I ask him to. And when he does, we aint never even gonna talk about you. Ni una palabra. We're gonna talk about the track or the weather or my new grandson or cualquiera chingada cosa que queremos, but we aint gonna talk about you. And we aint gonna talk about my son neither. I had a compadre before you went and mess it all up. So you can forget any other ideas you got, cuz everything's gonna go back to normal. Todo está bien arreglado. Y cuando te digo que my compadre's coming for dinner, you're gonna make his favorite chile verde. I don't care what you feel ¿m'entiendes? Me vas a obedecer. And you'll put the plate of food in front of his face and you'll pretend that you feel nothing, menos que antes. Becuz if I see you give him even a little sign, like your face gets a little red o demasiada pálida or your hand shakes a little when you pour el café into la taza, recuerdas que te estoy watchando, mujer. And it's gonna be like old times and you're not going to mess it up again.

He stuffs the letter he has written into an envelope and seals it. He puts both letters into his pocket and exits. HORTENSIA *sits, drops her face into her hands. Fade out.*

Scene Four

LUPE *is on the porch, shining* MANUEL's *shoes.* ROSARIO *approaches, sits on the step.*

ROSARIO: Tu papi's getting all spruced up, eh?

LUPE: Really.

ROSARIO: Dáme uno. Yo te ayudo.

LUPE: Thanks, tía. (ROSARIO *hands* LUPE *a shoe to polish.*)

ROSARIO: He's going out?

LUPE: Uh-huh.

ROSARIO: ¿A dónde?

LUPE: To see that man.

ROSARIO: Who?

LUPE: Conrado.

ROSARIO: How do you know?

LUPE: I heard papi telling mami. She's getting his clothes ready. She's been singing all day, so she won't say nuthin' mean to him.

ROSARIO: She's singing?

LUPE: She's mad inside, so she sings. That way only nice things come out of her mouth.

ROSARIO: Tu mamá es una buena mujer.

LUPE: I know.

HORTENSIA *enters the kitchen singing to herself. She puts a pair of* MANUEL's *dress pants and a suit coat over the back of a chair. She crosses to the ironing board, begins pressing his dress shirt.*

MANUEL (*offstage*): Lupe! ¡Los zapatos!

LUPE: I'm coming! (ROSARIO *and* LUPE *rise, go into the kitchen.*)

ROSARIO: If they dint take the license from me we could all go out and paint the town ourselves tonight.

LUPE: In that car! Forget it, tía! It's got fins sharp enough to kill somebody.

ROSARIO: Pues, we got pertection then.

LUPE *exits with the shoes.* ROSARIO *pours herself a cup of coffee and sits at the table.*

ROSARIO: Conrado's back?

HORTENSIA: Sí. (*Pause.*) It's like he wants to jump right into the heart of the herida and bury himself in there. I'm his wife, but I'm not gointu jump in there with him.

MANUEL *enters in boxer shorts and T-shirt, talking to himself softly. He wears a hat and holds his shoes and two ties.* HORTENSIA *hands him the shirt and he puts it on. The two women watch him dress in silence. He puts on the pants, examining its crease. He licks his fingers and runs them down the crease's edge. He sits down, then stands up, checking the crease again.*

MANUEL: The crease doesn't stay in them. (*He looks distraught, holds up the two ties.*) La azul or the yellow one?

HORTENSIA: La azul.

MANUEL *chooses the yellow one instead, stuffing the blue one into his pant pocket. He sits down and puts on his shoes with a shoehorn. The women continue watching him dress, their eyes never leaving him.*

ROSARIO: Sometimes a man thinks of another man before he thinks of nobody else. He don' think about his woman ni su madre ni los children, jus' what he gots in his head about tha' man. He closes his eyes and dreams, "If I could get inside tha' man, then I'd really be somebody!" But when he opens his eyes and sees that he's as empty as he was before, he curls his fingers into fists and knocks down whatever he thinks is standing in his way.

MANUEL *stands, buttons his coat, looks at* HORTENSIA.

HORTENSIA: If you go, Manuel, you won't find me here when you get back. I don't know where you'll find me, but I won't be here.

MANUEL: Fine. (*He starts for the door.*)

HORTENSIA: I'll take the girls, Manuel. You'll have a empty house to come home to. No 'stoy jugando. The minute you walk out that door.

MANUEL *turns around, crosses to her and kisses her on the cheek. She stares back at him.*

HORTENSIA: No puedo aguantarlo. No puedo.

MANUEL: You'll do as I say. Things will get better now. You'll see.

He goes to the door, dips his hat slightly over one eye and runs his fingers over the rim of it. He imagines himself a different man, in Conrado's image.

MANUEL: Adios, mujer.

He exits. The women stare at the door in silence.

HORTENSIA: I don't want Lupita here when Manuel comes home tonight.

ROSARIO: Sí, hermana. I'll take her.

LUPE (*reentering, suddenly frightened*): Tía?

HORTENSIA: You're gointu go with your tía tonight, mija.

LUPE: But . . .

HORTENSIA: Lettie will bring your piyamas later.

ROSARIO *puts her arm around* LUPE *to escort her out of the house.*

LUPE: Is it papi's friend, mami?

HORTENSIA: No. Everything's fine. You be a good girl now. Help your
    tía.

LUPE: Sí, mami.

ROSARIO: Good night, hermana. (*They go to the door.*)

HORTENSIA: Good night.

LUPE: Mami? . . .

HORTENSIA (*goes to* LUPE, *kisses her*): Nos vemos por la mañana, mija
    . . . muy tempranito.

LUPE *and* ROSARIO *exit. After a few moments,* HORTENSIA *goes out
onto the porch, lights a cigarette, waits.*

Scene Five

It is the wee hours of the morning. HORTENSIA *sits out on the porch.* LE-
TICIA *enters wearing a miniskirt and boots.* LETICIA *doesn't notice* HORTEN-
SIA *until she speaks.*

HORTENSIA: It's two o'clock in the morning.

LETICIA: I know. (LETICIA *goes into the kitchen.* HORTENSIA *follows
    her.*)

HORTENSIA: ¿Crees que eres mujer ya?

LETICIA: No.

HORTENSIA: Eres hombre, entonces. That's what you want, isn't it? To
    be free like a man.

LETICIA: That wouldn't be so bad.

HORTENSIA: Pues, no naciste varón. If God had wanted you to be a man, he would of given you something between your legs.

LETICIA: I have something between my legs.

HORTENSIA: Está bien. Then go wipe the streets with it if that's what you want!

LETICIA: Why do you gotta talk to me like that?

HORTENSIA: ¡Lárgate de esta casa! ¡Si no tienes respeto a tus padres, lárgate! There's the door, señorita.

LETICIA: I can see it. (*She goes to the cupboard, finds a shopping bag.*)

HORTENSIA: ¿A dónde vas?

LETICIA: Just obeying you, mamá.

HORTENSIA: Go 'head. You think your pachuco boyfriend loves you so much?

LETICIA: No.

HORTENSIA: Pues, go to him. But he'll kick you out in the street, too. He knows what you are.

LETICIA: And what am I, mamá? Díme. What am I?

HORTENSIA: Desgraciada!

LETICIA: ¿Como tú?

HORTENSIA (*grabbing the bag from her*): Maybe better I should of cut Lupita out from me! That would of made all you santos happy . . . that I would cut your sister from me and nobody had to know the difernce.

LETICIA: Mamá.

HORTENSIA: Well, I can tell you one thing, mujer, I don' give a damn who sticks their thing inside me, that doesn't make a father. What comes out of me is my own flesh and blood! The father is the one who puts the food on the table, nomás.

LETICIA (*softly*): I know that.

HORTENSIA *lights up another cigarette, sits at the table and for a few moments smokes in silence.*

LETICIA: Mamá?

HORTENSIA: Do you think I was never young? I know what you're feeling and I can't stop you. You walk in that door and I can smell the woman coming out of you.

LETICIA: What's wrong with that?

HORTENSIA: Maybe there's nothing wrong with that. I don' know what to tell you no more. What consejo can I give you? I marry un hombre tranquilo, a good man. And I watch his back bend, his belly blow up with beer and I see my own daughter grow to look at him con desprecio and . . . contempt.

LETICIA: It's not contempt, mamá. It's pity.

HORTENSIA: That's worse.

There is a pause. LETICIA *goes downstage, stands with her back to* HORTENSIA.

LETICIA: I thought of you tonight. I thought of no longer being your daughter, that what I was gonna do would turn you away from me.

HORTENSIA: I don' wannu know.

LETICIA: There they were, the Raza gods with their legs spread, popping beers, talking revolución and those things, each with its own life, its own personality and I wanted to taste them all. Each and every fruta. "Una joya," you would say. (*Pause.*) So, I opened my legs to one of them, mamá. The way a person opens her arms to take the whole world in, I opened my legs.

HORTENSIA: Is that what you call love?

LETICIA (*turning to her*): It's not about love. It's power. Power we get to hold and caress and protect. Power they drop into our hands, so fragile the slightest pressure makes them weak with pain.

HORTENSIA: Why, mija? Why you give your virginidad away for nothing?

LETICIA: I was tired of carrying it around, that weight of being a woman with a prize. Walking around with that special secret, that valuable commodity, waiting for some lucky guy to put his name on it. I wanted it to be worthless, mamá. Don't you see? Not for me to be worthless, but to know that my worth had nothing to do with it.

HORTENSIA (*after a pause*): You protect yourself, hija?

LETICIA: Yeah. I'll be all right.

After a pause, HORTENSIA *goes to her. They embrace.* HORTENSIA's *anguished face can be seen over* LETICIA's *shoulder.* LETICIA *exits upstage.*

Scene Six

Crossfade to CONRADO *entering the garden. The lighting assumes a dream-like, surreal quality. Action seems to occur outside of time.* CONRADO *is well dressed in a double-breasted, '40s-style suit and wears a hat dipped over one eye.* HORTENSIA *sits in the kitchen, still waiting for* MANUEL's *return. As* CONRADO *goes up the porch steps, he removes his hat, combs his hair with his fingers, replaces the hat. At the same moment,* HORTENSIA *takes off her bathrobe. She wears a dark evening dress. She goes to the door.*

HORTENSIA: ¿Dónde 'stá Manuel?

CONRADO: He told me to go on ahead. He's not here yet?

HORTENSIA: No. (*Pause.*) Pásale. (CONRADO *enters.*)

CONRADO: Te ves igual.

HORTENSIA: After thirteen years?

CONRADO: You look the same.

HORTENSIA: ¿Y tú? Are you the same?

CONRADO: Pues, díme. Am I?

HORTENSIA: You've changed.

CONRADO: I'm older. (*He laughs.*)

　　　They both sit.

HORTENSIA (*after a pause*): Why did you come back?

CONRADO: To see Manuel. (*Pause.*) He wrote me.

HORTENSIA: Ya lo sé.

CONRADO: He told you?

HORTENSIA: Sí

CONRADO: He said you wanted me to come back.

HORTENSIA: And you believe that?

CONRADO: No sé. (*Pause.*) I'm broke.

HORTENSIA: That's why you came back?

CONRADO: Pues . . .

HORTENSIA: So, you didn't make it so big?

CONRADO: No, 'mana.

　　　They both smile.

HORTENSIA: So, here you are.

CONRADO: Here I am. (*Pause.*) You remember one morning, I was standing on the corner of First and Figueroa. I was with a woman, una güera, muy alta. I was talking to her when I heard the streetcar go pass behind me. I turned around and I saw you looking at me through the window. The sun was just coming up into our eyes. And I turned to la güera y la bese en la boca.

HORTENSIA: Yo recuerdo.

CONRADO: I did that to let you go, so that you would go to him. Barely a month later and you married Manuel. (*Pause.*) He never knew what he had.

HORTENSIA: He's been good to me.

CONRADO (*after a pause*): In those early days I used to watch Riguito and Leticia circling around you in the kitchen. Two little satellites in your orbit. I watched the way you moved inside your apron. I wanted you, Tencha.

HORTENSIA: No me digas más. (*She stands. "Sunrise Serenade" by Glen Miller rises in the background.*) When we first met, you and Manuel and me . . . we had a good time, the three of us. He was the one I was with, but I was proud of you both, tan guapos en sus uniformes. Manuel would dance a few numbers with me and then he'd say, "This one's for you, 'mano. Dance with Tencha."

CONRADO *goes to* HORTENSIA, *takes her into his arms and they dance.* MANUEL *appears upstage in shadow, watching.* CONRADO *dips* HORTENSIA *and is about to kiss her, she turns her face away.* CONRADO *spies* MANUEL.

CONRADO: Compadre.

HORTENSIA *backs away.*

MANUEL (*to* CONRADO): You never have enough. What I gave you was never enough.

CONRADO: Nothing happened.

MANUEL: ¿Ahora quieres más, compadre? It's not enough you come back to pick my pocket without a dime in your own?

CONRADO: Manuel, I didn't—

MANUEL: "There she is waiting for you, compadre." Isn't that what I said? "I'll give you the shirt off my back." You want my shirt? (*He starts unbuttoning his shirt.*)

CONRADO: Stop it, compa.

MANUEL: You want my hat? (*He shoves* CONRADO *into a chair, removes* CONRADO's *hat and sticks his own hat on him.*) How about la waifa?

MANUEL *grabs* HORTENSIA *and throws her onto* CONRADO's *lap. She crawls away.*

MANUEL: After you left her como un trapo en la cama, how was I suppose to go to her? Wipe up the little that you left of her. She walked around the house like she was something special, like she (*He grabs* CONRADO *by the balls.*) got a piece of you. You know what that feels like? To have your own wife hold something inside her que no es tuyo? She made me feel like I was nothing. (*Pause.*) I loved you, man. I gave you hasta mi propia mujer, but that didn't mean nothing to you. You just went and left. I gave you my fucking wife, cabrón. What does that make me? (*Pause.*) And all these years she looks at me like she knows something I don't know, like she's got something I don't got.

HORTENSIA: Manuel, a mí no me puedes echar la culpa. You were there that night. I heard you both coming in, laughing and crying. Conrado was leaving. And then I fell off to sleep, but when I open my eyes again, the whole house está bien bien quieto y veo esta sombra in the doorway.

CONRADO *slowly moves toward* HORTENSIA. *He comes up behind her.*

HORTENSIA: You stand there in the dark sin decir nada, jus' staring at me. You come and lay down next to me. (CONRADO *puts his arms around her.*) Pones la mano around my waist and your touch is difernt. Hablas . . .

CONRADO: Hortensia.

HORTENSIA: And it's not your voice. I tell you que te vayas, that we can't do what you're thinking. Y me respondes . . .

CONRADO: No te apures. Manuel knows. This is what he wants.

HORTENSIA: Y cierro los ojos, and I wrap myself around you, and nothing is the same after that. (*Pause.*) Leave us alone now, compadre.

CONRADO *hesitates, looking at them each for a moment, then grabs his hat and exits. There is a pause.* HORTENSIA *reaches her arms out to* MANUEL *in a final gesture to him. He turns his face away. She exits.*

MANUEL *sits in a stupor alone in the room. He slowly rises, takes out a fresh fifth of tequila and a bottle of pills. He swallows half the pills, washing them down with the tequila.*

MANUEL: Lupita! (*He goes toward the bedroom.*) She's waiting for me. (*He enters the bedroom. When he doesn't see her, he begins to panic.*) Lupe? Lupita! (*He rushes back into the kitchen.*) She's gone! ¡Miji-i-i-ta!

He slumps into the chair and begins to cry. It is a kind of labored sobbing of a man unable to reach the core of his despair.

MANUEL: She took from me everything I ever loved.

Moments later, he composes himself, his face hardened, impassive. He grabs the bottle of tequila and goes out onto the porch. The sun is beginning to rise. He sits, a silhouette against the dawn's light, swallows the remainder of the pills and raises the bottle to his lips. He drinks the entire bottle down, his head thrown back. Black out. In the dark, there is the sound of his body hitting the floor.

Moments later, the lights rise to reveal MANUEL *in a heap on the floor.* HORTENSIA *enters, rushes to him, puts her ear to his heart. She looks up in horror. Black out.*

Scene Seven

LUPE *stands in her robe in front of the bathroom mirror, a rosary with crucifix in her hand. She lights a candle as at the beginning of the play, then takes out the photo of Conrado her father had left. She studies the image for a moment, measuring it against her own reflection in the mirror. Then she tears the small photo into pieces and drops it into the mouth of the burning candle. The shadow of the crucifix goes up in flames. Fade out.*

Scene Eight

The day of MANUEL's *funeral. The women are gathered in the Rodríguez kitchen.* HORTENSIA *is ironing a black dress.* ROSARIO *mends a black rebozo.* LETICIA *is painting her fingernails.* LUPE *enters, joins her sister and aunt at the table.*

ROSARIO: Bueno, somos puras hembras now. A house full of women nomás.

They look at one another, as if noticing for the first time.

HORTENSIA: I wish it were all over already. (*She hands* LETICIA *the dress.*)

LETICIA (*blowing on her nails*): Thanks, Mom.

HORTENSIA (*with affection*): And do something about your hair. I don' wan' it wild como una india.

ROSARIO: Ven, mija. Te hago una trenza. I got a nice cinta for it.

LETICIA: All right.

LETICIA *and* ROSARIO *exit upstage.* HORTENSIA *begins to iron* LUPITA's *dress.*

LUPE (*after a pause*): Did you love papi, mami?

HORTENSIA (*after a pause*): No sé. To be with a man so long, day in and day out, it's hard to know. Your head on the pillow next to his. You feel his body, his weight, su aliento. I could know tu padre's breathing anywhere porque lo oigo hasta en mis sueños. Entra en el alma cuando uno duerme. (*Pause.*) Funny, when a man is asleep, that's when you really get to know him. You see the child's look on his face, before he wakes up and remembers he's a man again. ¿Sabes qué, mija? Tu papi siempre se despertaba con la voz de un niño.

LUPE: ¿Un niño?

HORTENSIA: He sound jus' like a little boy. (*Pause.*) Después de tantos años, es difícil decir, "He dug his own grave, let him lie in it." I know I could never do that with you children. No matter what you did, you would always be my children.

LUPE: Even Rigo, mami?

HORTENSIA: Of course, even Rigo. With a husband, it's difernt. You see, this man did not come from your body. No matter cuantas veces le das la chichi, tu marido no es tu hijo. Your blood never mixes. He stays a stranger in his own home. (*She gives* LUPE *the dress.*) Andale, mijita. You better get dressed. Rigo will be here para llevarnos purty soon.

LUPE: All right, mami.

LUPE *exits to the bathroom. She dresses.* LETICIA *enters with a suitcase as* CONRADO *approaches the porch. He holds a note in his hand. He removes his hat, combs his hair back with his fingers.* LETICIA *gives* HORTENSIA *the suitcase.*

LETICIA: It's Conrado.

HORTENSIA: Did I kill him? When you let go your child's hand and they go off to meet la Muerte in the street, es tu culpa? Or es el destino?

LETICIA *exits.* HORTENSIA *goes to the door.*

CONRADO (*referring to the note*): You wanted me to get his things?

HORTENSIA: Aquí 'stá su ropa. (*She gives him the suitcase.*)

CONRADO: What should I do with them?

HORTENSIA: Wear them. Burn them.

CONRADO *exits. Sound of car pulling up.* ROSARIO *enters.*

ROSARIO: Ya es hora. Ha llegado Rigo.

HORTENSIA: Lupe!

LUPE: I'm coming.

The three women begin to file out. ROSARIO *stops, crosses to the table, picks up the rebozo, and goes to* LUPE.

ROSARIO (*handing her the rebozo*): Lupita, cover up ese espejo. We don' wan' your papi to come back and try and take us with him.

LUPE: Sí, señora.

The women exit in procession. LUPE *starts to cover the mirror, then pauses for a moment before her reflection.*

LUPE: I've decided my confirmation name will be Frances cuz that's what Frankie Pacheco's name is and I wannu be in her body. When she sits, she doesn't hold her knees together like my mom and the nuns are always telling me to. She jus' lets them fly and fall wherever they want, real natural-like, like they was wings instead of knees. (*Pause.*) And she's got a laugh, a laugh that seems to come from way deep inside herself, from the bottom of her heart or something. (*Pause.*) If I could, I'd like to jus' unzip her chest and climb right inside there, next to her heart, to feel everything she's feeling and I could forget about me. (*Pause.*) It's okay if she doesn't feel the same way, . . . it's my secret.

HORTENSIA (*offstage*): Lupe!

LUPE: Ya voy.

She covers the mirror with the rebozo. The lights fade to black.

End

Heroes and Saints

Before day breaks we shall
set out from these yards and
reach their city . . . in the dawn
showing in public places the full extent of our misery
appealing to anything with a human look.
What will come after, I don't know.

St. Joan of the Stockyards

"Aztlán belongs to those who plant the seeds,
water the fields, and gather the crops . . ."

For Aztlán's Children

Heroes and Saints had its world premiere on April 4, 1992, at El Teatro Misión of San Francisco, produced by Brava! For Women in the Arts under the artistic direction of Ellen Gavin. It included the following cast (in order of appearance):

Cerezita Valle	Jaime Lujan
Dolores	Juanita Estrada
Ana Pérez	Charo Toledo
Amparo	Viola Lucero
Bonnie	Anna Marina Bensaud
Yolanda	Jennifer Proctor
Mario	Angelo Pagán
Father Juan	Hector Correa
Don Gilberto	Gary Martínez

It was directed by Albert Takazauckas, with sets by Barbara Mesney and Birch Thomas, lighting design by Kurt Landisman, sound design by Maurice Tani, and visual design installation by Estér Hernández.

Heroes and Saints was initially commissioned through José Luis Valenzuela's Latino Lab of the Los Angeles Theatre Center and was performed as a staged reading on October 7, 1989, under the direction of José Guadalupe Saucedo. The play was also presented in the Latin American Theatre Artist Staged Reading Series in San Francisco on April 28, 29, and 30, 1991, under the direction of the author.

AUTHOR'S NOTES

Although *Heroes and Saints* is fiction, it came in response to the numerous events that took place in 1988 which brought growing visibility to the United Farm Workers' grape boycott in protest against pesticide poisoning. The greatest public attention came as a result of the 36-day fast by the president of the union, Cesar Chávez, which ended on August 21, 1988. Less than a month later, the vice-president of the union, Dolores Huerta, was brutally beaten by a San Francisco policeman while holding a press conference protesting George Bush's refusal to honor the boycott.

Behind the scenes of these events are the people whose personal tragedy inspired a national political response. In the town of McFarland in the San Joaquin Valley of California, a so-called cancer cluster was discovered. Within a ten-year period from 1978 to 1988, a highly disproportionate number of children were diagnosed with cancer and were born with birth defects. After viewing the UFW's documentary video *The Wrath of Grapes*, which describes the McFarland situation, an image remained in my mind—a child with no arms or legs, born of a farm worker mother. The mother had been picking in pesticide-sprayed fields while her baby was still in the womb. This child became Cerezita, a character who came to me when I wondered of the child's future as we turn into the next century.

I want to thank Luis Valdez for his play *The Shrunken Head of Pancho Villa*, whose head character became, for me, a point of departure. I also wish to thank El Teatro Campesino for allowing me access to their archives on the McFarland situation. I am indebted to Marta Salinas, a mother and one of the chief organizers in McFarland, who opened her home and the homes of other McFarland families to me. The character of Doña Amparo is my tribute to her, as it is to Dolores Huerta, a woman whose courage and relentless commitment to Chicano/a freedom has served as a source of inspiration to two generations of Chicanas.

Finally, I dedicate this play to the memory and legacy of Cesar Chávez.

CHARACTERS

CEREZITA VALLE, *the head*
AMPARO, *the comadre and activista*
ANA PEREZ, *the news reporter*
DOLORES, *the mother*
BONNIE, *a neighbor's child "adopted" by* AMPARO *and* DON GILBERTO
YOLANDA, *the hairdresser sister*
MARIO, *the sometimes-student brother*
FATHER JUAN, *the "half-breed" leftist priest*
DON GILBERTO, *the compadre,* AMPARO's *husband*
POLICEMAN
EL PUEBLO, *the children and mothers of McLaughlin;* THE PEOPLE / PRO-
    TESTORS / AUDIENCE *participating in the struggle (ideally,* EL PUEBLO
    should be made up of an ensemble of people from the local Latino community)

Notes on CEREZITA

CEREZITA *is a head of human dimension, but one who possesses such dignity of bearing and classical Indian beauty she can, at times, assume nearly religious proportions. (The huge head figures of the pre-Columbian Olmecas are an apt comparison.) This image, however, should be contrasted with the very real "humanness" she exhibits on a daily functioning level. Her mobility and its limits are critical aspects of her character. For most of the play,* CEREZITA *is positioned on a rolling, tablelike platform, which will be referred to as her "raite" (ride). It is automated by a button she operates with her chin. The low hum of its motor always anticipates her entrance. The raite can be disengaged at any time by flipping the hold on each wheel and pushing the chin piece out of her reach. At such times,* CEREZITA *has no control and can only be moved by someone manually.*

SETTING

The play takes place in McLaughlin, California, a fictional town in the San Joaquin Valley. The year is 1988.

McLaughlin is a one-exit town off Highway 99. On the east side of the highway sits the old part of town, consisting primarily of a main street of three blocks of small businesses—the auto supply store, a small supermarket, the post office, a laundromat, an old central bank with a recently added automatic teller machine, a storefront Iglesia de Dios and, of course, a video movie rental shop. Crossing the two-lane bridge over Highway 99, a new McLaughlin has emerged. From the highest point of the overpass, a large island of single-family stucco houses and apartments can be seen. The tracts were built in the late '70s and reflect a manicured uniformity in appearance, each house with its obligatory crew-cut lawn and one-step front porch. Surrounding the island is an endless sea of agricultural fields which, like the houses, have been perfectly arranged into neatly juxtaposed rectangles.

The hundreds of miles of soil that surround the lives of Valley dwellers should not be confused with land. What was once land has become dirt, overworked dirt, overirrigated dirt, injected with deadly doses of chemicals and violated by every manner of ground- and back-breaking machinery. The people that worked the dirt do not call what was once the land their enemy. They remember what land used to be and await its second coming.

To that end, the grape vineyards, pecan tree orchards and the endless expanse of the Valley's agricultural life should be constant presences in the play and visibly press upon the intimate life of the Valle family home. The relentless fog and sudden dramatic sunbreaks in the Valley sky physically alter the mood of each scene. The Valle family home is modest in furnishing but always neat, and looks onto EL PUEBLO through a downstage window. Scenes outside the family home can be represented by simple, movable set pieces, e.g., a park bench for the street scenes, a wheelchair for the hospital, a set of steps for the church, etc.

ACT I

Scene One

At rise in the distance, a group of children wearing calavera masks enters the grape vineyard. They carry a small, child-size cross which they erect quickly and exit, leaving its stark silhouetted image against the dawn's light. The barely distinguishable figure of a small child hangs from it. The child's hair and thin clothing flap in the wind. Moments pass. The wind subsides. The sound of squeaking wheels and a low, mechanical hum interrupt the silence. CEREZITA enters in shadow. She is transfixed by the image of the crucifixion. The sun suddenly explodes out of the horizon, bathing both the child and CEREZITA. CEREZITA is awesome and striking in the light. The crucified child glows, Christlike. The sound of a low-flying helicopter invades the silence. Its shadow passes over the field. Black out.

Scene Two

Mexican rancheras can be heard coming from a small radio in the Valle home. ANA PEREZ is on the street in front of the house. She holds a microphone and is expertly made up. AMPARO, a stocky woman in her fifties, is digging holes in the yard next door. She wears heavy-duty rubber gloves.

ANA PEREZ (*to the "cameraman"*): Bob, is my hair okay? What? . . . I have lipstick? Where? Here? (*She wets her finger with her tongue, rubs the corner of her lip.*) Okay? . . . Good. (*Addressing the "camera."*) Hello, I'm Ana Pérez and this is another edition of our Channel Five news special: "Hispanic California." Today I am speaking to you from the town of McLaughlin in the San Joaquin Valley. McLaughlin is commonly believed to be a cancer cluster area, where a disproportionate number of children have been diagnosed with cancer in the last few years. The town has seen the sudden death of numerous children, as well as a high incidence of birth defects. One of the most alarming recent events which has brought sudden public attention to the McLaughlin situation has been a series of . . . crucifixions, performed in what seems to be a kind of ritualized protest against the dying of McLaughlin children. (DOLORES, *a slender woman nearing fifty, enters. She carries groceries.*) The last three children to die were each found with his corpse hanging from a cross in the middle of a grape vineyard. The Union of Campesinos, an outspoken advocate for pesticide control, is presently under investigation for the crime. (*Spying* DOLORES.) We now are approaching the house of Dolores Valle. Her daughter Cerezita is one of McLaughlin's most tragic cases.

Upon sight of ANA PEREZ *coming toward her with her microphone,* DOLORES *hurries into the house.* AMPARO *intervenes.*

AMPARO: You should maybe leave her alone; she don' like the telebision cameras too much no more.

ANA PEREZ (*to the "camera"*): Possibly this neighbor can provide us with some sense of the emotional climate prevalent in this small, largely Hispanic farm worker town.

AMPARO: She says es como un circo—

ANA PEREZ (*to the camera*): A circus.

AMPARO: Que la gente . . . the peepo like tha' kina t'ing, to look at somebody else's life like that t'ing coont never happen to them. But Cerezita's big now. She got a lot to say if they give her the chance. It's important for the peepo to reelize what los rancheros—

ANA PEREZ (*overlapping*): The growers.

AMPARO: Are doing to us.

ANA PEREZ: Cerezita. That's an unusual name. Es una fruta ¿qué no?

AMPARO: That's what they call her because she look like tha' . . . a red little round cherry face. I think maybe all the blood tha' was apose to go to the resta her body got squeezed up into her head. I think tha's why she's so smart, too. Mario, her brother, el doctor-to-be, says the blood gots oxygen. Tha's gottu help with the brains. So pink pink pink she turn out.

ANA PEREZ: And how old is Cerezita now?

AMPARO: A big teenager already. Cerezita come out like this before anybody think too much about it. Now there's lotza nuevas because lotza kids are turning out all chuecos and with ugly things growing inside them. So our pueblito, pues it's on the map now. The gabachos, s'cuze me, los americanos are always coming through McLaughlin nowdays. Pero, not too much change. We still can' prove it's those chemcals they put on the plantas. But we know Cere turn out this way because Dolores pick en los files cuando tenía panza.

ANA PEREZ: Uh . . . pregnant, I think.

AMPARO: Dolores tells me que no le importa a la gente and maybe she's right. She says all the publeesty gives peepo somet'ing to do. Peepo que got a lotta free time. It gives them a purpose, she says—like God.

ANA PEREZ: Señora, what about the boy?

AMPARO: ¿Qué boy?

ANA PEREZ: The boy on the cross . . . in the field.

AMPARO: Memo?

ANA PEREZ: Yes. Memo Delgado.

AMPARO: He died a little santito, son angelitos todos.

ANA PEREZ: That's the third one.

AMPARO: Yes.

ANA PEREZ: Why would someone be so cruel, to hang a child up like that? To steal him from his deathbed?

AMPARO: No, he was dead already. Already dead from the poison.

ANA PEREZ: But ma'am . . .

AMPARO: They always dead first. If you put the children in the ground, the world forgets about them. Who's gointu see them, buried in the dirt?

ANA PEREZ: A publicity stunt? But who's—

AMPARO: Señorita, I don' know who. But I know they not my enemy. (*Beat.*) Con su permiso. (AMPARO *walks away.*)

ANA PEREZ (*with false bravado*): That concludes our Hispanic hour for the week, but watch for next week's show where we will take a five-hour drive north to the heart of San Francisco's Latino Mission District, for an insider's observation of the Day of the Dead, the Mexican Halloween. (*She holds a television smile for three full seconds. To the "cameraman":*) Cut! We'll edit her out later.

BONNIE *and a group of small* CHILDREN *enter wearing calavera masks. They startle her.*

THE CHILDREN: Trick or treat!

ANA PEREZ: No. I mean . . . I don't . . . have anything to give you.

She exits nervously.

Scene Three

Crossfade to the Valle kitchen. It is late afternoon. YOLANDA *is breastfeeding her baby.* CEREZITA *observes.*

CEREZITA: I remember the first time I tasted fear, I smelled it in her sweat. It ran like a tiny river down her breast and mixed with her milk. I tasted it on my tongue. It was very bitter. Very bitter.

YOLANDA: That's why I try to keep calm. Lina knows when I'm upset.

CEREZITA: I stopped drinking. I refused to nurse from her again, bit at her breasts when she tried to force me.

YOLANDA: Formula is expensive. Breastfeeding is free. Healthier, too. I'll do it until Lina doesn't want it no more. (YOLANDA *buttons her blouse, puts the infant into her crib, sings to her softly.*) 'Duerme, duerme, negrito' . . . (*Continues singing.*)

CEREZITA: But imagine my sadness, my longing for the once-sweetness of her nipple.

YOLANDA *positions* CEREZITA *for her weekly beauty treatment. She takes out various beauty supplies from a bag.* MARIO *enters, towel wrapped around his hips. He is well built, endearingly macho in his manner. He is drying himself briskly.*

MARIO: ¡Hijo! It's freezing! These cold showers suck, man! We should all just get the fuck outta here. I'm gonna move us all the fuck outta here!

CEREZITA: Where to, Mario?

YOLANDA: Go 'head, chulo. You keep taking those showers purty boy and your skin's gonna fall off in sheets. Then who's gonna want you?

MARIO: The water was cold, man. Ice cold.

YOLANDA: I turned the water heater off.

MARIO: Great. My skin's gonna freeze off from the cold sooner than any chemicals. How can you stand it?

CEREZITA: Where you gonna move us to, Mario?

MARIO (*looking out the window*): What?

CEREZITA: Where we going?

MARIO: I dunno. Just away.

YOLANDA (*has filled up a glass of water from the faucet*): Here.

MARIO: Chale. The shit stinks.

YOLANDA: C'mon, chulo. Tómalo. Why don't you just throw it down your throat better? It's the same thing. You suck enough of it up through your skin taking those hot baths three times a day.

MARIO: Two.

YOLANDA *starts to spread the beauty mask onto* CEREZITA's *face.* DOLORES *can be seen coming up the porch steps after her day's work.*

YOLANDA: You wanna see Lina's nalguitas? They're fried, man. The hot water opens your pores and just sucks up the stuff. She cried all night last night. This shit's getting outta hand! Doña Amparo told me—

DOLORES (*entering*): Es una metiche, Amparo.

YOLANDA: They shot through her windows the last night.

CEREZITA: Who?

YOLANDA: Who knows? The guys in the helicopters . . . God.

DOLORES: Por eso, te digo she better learn to keep her damn mouth shut. Ella siempre gottu be putting la cuchara en la olla. I saw her talking to the TV peepo last week right in front of the house. It scare me.

YOLANDA: What are you scared of?

DOLORES: They come to talk to Amparo on the job yesterday.

MARIO: Who?

DOLORES: The patrones.

MARIO: The owners?

DOLORES: Not the owners, pero their peepo. They give her a warning que they don' like her talking about the rancheros.

YOLANDA: Cabrones.

DOLORES: She gointu lose her job.

MARIO: Got to hand it to Nina Amparo. She's got huevos, man.

DOLORES: She got a husband, not huevos. Who's gointu support Cere if I stop working?

The room falls silent. CERE's *face is now covered in a facial mask.*

MARIO: Well, I better get ready. (*He starts to exit upstage,* DOLORES *stops him.*)

DOLORES: I better see you back el lunes temprano ¿m'oyes? I got the plaster falling down from the front of the house.

MARIO: Okay.

CEREZITA: Where you going, Mario?

DOLORES *goes to the stove, puts a pot of beans to boil.*

YOLANDA: Don't talk, Cere. You're gonna crack your face.

MARIO: ¡San Pancho, 'manita!

YOLANDA (*running a slab of facial down his cheek, softly*): Better stay away from the jotos, you don't wanna catch nothing.

MARIO (*"slabbing" it back, teasing*): I got it covered, hermana.

DOLORES: What are you two whispering about?

MARIO: Nothing, 'amá.

DOLORES: You know, secrets kill sometimes.

YOLANDA: It was nothing, 'amá.

DOLORES: You don' believe it, pero tha' place, it's crazy. They got all those crazy peepo que sleep on the street nowdays. You never know one could come up and shoot you right in the head.

YOLANDA: They're shooting us here anyway.

DOLORES: ¿Crees que soy una exagerada? We'll see.

MARIO (*mimicking*): "We'll see." ¡Hijo! I hate when she says that like she knows something we don't.

YOLANDA: I know.

DOLORES: Pues, maybe I do.

MARIO (*coming up behind DOLORES and wrapping his arms around her*): I'm fine, 'amá.

DOLORES (*softening*): "I'm fine, 'amá." ¿Qué sabes tú about "fine"?

AMPARO *can be seen coming up onto the porch. JUAN trails behind her carrying a five-gallon tank of spring water. He wears jeans and a flannel shirt.*

AMPARO: ¡Halo! Anybody home? I got a sorprise for you!

DOLORES: Abra la puerta, hijo.

AMPARO (*calling out behind her*): Right here! This is the house!

MARIO (*going to the door*): What's up, Nina?

AMPARO: ¡Ay! Te vez bien sexy.

DOLORES (*spying JUAN at the porch*): ¡Ay, Dios! (*She quickly pushes CERE-ZITA out of sight, drawing a curtain around her.*)

YOLANDA (*whispering*): Why do you do that to her?

DOLORES: Cállete tú.

MARIO (*to* JUAN, *with interest*): Hello.

JUAN: Hello.

AMPARO: This is my godson, Mario. (MARIO *takes the bottle from* JUAN.)

JUAN: Thanks.

MARIO: No problem.

AMPARO: That's Yolanda y su baby, Evalina.

YOLANDA: Hi.

AMPARO: And this is my comadre, Dolores Valle.

DOLORES: Halo.

JUAN: Mucho gusto.

DOLORES: ¿Habla español?

JUAN: Soy mexicano.

DOLORES: ¿Verdad?

AMPARO (*aside*): Half y half.

MARIO (*suggestively*): Like the cream?

AMPARO: And a priest. Father Juan Cunningham.

DOLORES: Mario, why you standing around sin ropa? Go put some clothes on.

MARIO: All right. I was just helping the man. I mean, the priest.

He puts the water onto the dispenser, then exits. JUAN's *eyes follow him.*

DOLORES: Siéntese, Father.

YOLANDA: So, where'd you get the water, Doña Amparo?

AMPARO: The Arrowhead donated it.

JUAN: Thanks to Doña Amparo. Last week's newscast stirred up everyone!

AMPARO: It wasn' me. It was la crucifixión. That's what brought the newspeepo here.

DOLORES: ¡Es una barbaridad!

AMPARO: The newspeepo, they wanted to talk to Cereza, comadre.

DOLORES: Y ¿por qué?

YOLANDA: Cere knows, 'amá.

DOLORES: Cerezita don' know nothing.

YOLANDA: She sees.

DOLORES: She sees nothing. (*To* JUAN:) She looks out the window all day, nomás. What can she see?

The lights crossfade to CEREZITA *at the window.* BONNIE *sits near her, playing with a doll. She prepares bandages for it, tearing a flour-sack cloth into strips and wrapping it around the doll's head.*

CEREZITA: The sheep drink the same water we do from troughs outside my window. Today it is an orange-yellow color. The mothers dip their heads into the long rusty buckets and drink and drink while their babies deform inside them. Innocent, they sleep inside the same poison water and are born broken like me, their lamb limbs curling under them.

BONNIE (*takes out a thermometer and puts it into her doll's mouth*): ¿Estás malita, mija? (*Checking the temperature.*) Yes. I think you got "it." (*She rubs the top of its head, chanting.*)

'Sana sana colita de rana, si no sanas hoy sanarás mañana.
Sana sana colita de rana, si no sanas hoy sanarás mañana.
Sana sana colita de rana, si no sanas hoy sanarás mañana.'

She puts the doll into a small box and covers it tenderly with the remains of the cloth.

CEREZITA: I watch them from my window and weep.

Fade out.

Scene Four

DOLORES *and* JUAN *are at the kitchen table. He is eating a taco of chorizo. She embroiders a dishcloth.*

DOLORES: And then I started working in the packing houses and the same thing was happening. The poison they put on the almonds, it would make you sick. The women would run out of the place coz they had to throw up. Sure, I dint wannu go back in there, pero after awhile you start to accept it because you gottu have a job.

JUAN: Where do you work now?

DOLORES: Otro packing house. (*Pause.*) ¿Le gusta la comida, Father?

JUAN: Sí, está muy sabrosa.

DOLORES: Pues, I'm glad you came. Most a the priests, they not like you, they don' come to the house no more unless you got money. It's not right, Padre.

JUAN: No, no es justo, Señora Valle.

DOLORES: But the priests should be worried because a lot a peepo they leaving la iglesia. ¿Sabe qué? A buncha my vecinos already turn into the "Holy Rollie."

JUAN: Holy Rollie?

DOLORES: Tha's what my Yolie calls them. They turn from the Catholic god. They "Chrishins" now.

JUAN: Oh, you mean Pentecostals.

DOLORES: One time I was feeling so tire, so lonely, just dragging myself home from work and I hear a tamborín coming out of the panadería. Now it's a church, but it usetu be la panadería de la familia Hernández. It still smell like pandulce un poco when you go by. An' it was like the tamborín me 'staba llamando, telling me to come inside, if only para quitarme el cansancio a little. So I go in and sit in the back. And they were all jumping up and down and shaking their hands in the air. Pura raza, singing songs like children. It scare me, Father. Their faces look kina dopey-like, kina like their eyes had turned to hard glass por las lágrimas que tienen all lock up inside them. Se llama "Iglesia de Dios," but there wasn' no God there. And too much noise. How can your soul even find God con tanto ruído?

JUAN: I guess they feel they find him with one another.

DOLORES: No es posible. God es una cosa privada, un secreto que guardas and nobody can touch that part of you. Even the priest has to forget every secret you tell him. (*She observes* JUAN *as he finishes the dripping taco. He licks his fingers.*) ¡Ay, qué pena! (*She brings him a clean dishtowel.*) You been a father a long time, Father?

JUAN: About ten years.

DOLORES: You still have the eyes of a man.

JUAN: ¿Perdón?

DOLORES: No importa. It's good you experience the world a little. Some of these priests, you confess to them your sins y que consejo te pueben ofrecer? A little life doesn' hurt nobody. (*Pause.*) Come see my Cerezita. She'll like you. It's been years since a priest come to see her.

JUAN: Would you like me to hear her confession?

DOLORES: What sins could a girl like her have, Padre? She was born this way. Es una santa. We should pray to her, I think.

They both rise.

Crossfade to CEREZITA *speaking into a tape recorder.*

CEREZITA: It is so, he came to meet her seeking the purity of nature he'd lost. He sought baptism in the fire of her original desire.

JUAN (*entering timidly*): Hello . . . (CEREZITA *turns the tape recorder off with her chin.*) Am I . . . interrupting? (*She doesn't respond.*) Your mother asked me to come by. I hope it's . . . all right with you?

CEREZITA: She must like you. Few people get past her inspection.

JUAN: Can you turn around? I'd like to talk to you face to face.

CEREZITA: You're wasting your time, Padre. I have no use for God.

JUAN: You don't believe?

CEREZITA: I don't care.

JUAN: I see (*Pause.*) Can I read you something? Your mother says you are quite a reader.

CEREZITA (*reluctantly*): What is it?

JUAN: Just something I'm reading. It struck me.

CEREZITA: I got ears.

JUAN (*reading from a small paperback*): "Then, they named rich the man of God, and poor the man of flesh. And they determined that the rich would care for and protect the poor in as much that through them, the rich had received such benefits."

CEREZITA: "Entonces llamaron rico al hombre de oro y pobre al hombre de carne. Y dispusieron que el rico cuidara y amparara al pobre por cuanto que de él había recibido beneficios." . . .

JUAN (*impressed*): "And they ordered that the poor would respond on behalf of the rich before the face of truth."

CEREZITA: "Y ordenaron que el pobre respondería por el rico ante la cara de la verdad." . . .

JUAN: "For this—"

CEREZITA (*slowly turning to him*): "For this reason our law states that no rich person can enter heaven without the poor taking him by the hand."

Seeing her fully for the first time, JUAN's *face registers both awe and tenderness.*

JUAN: Balun Canan. Rosario Castellanos.

CEREZITA: First, the Maya. (*Pause.*) Am I your pobre, Father?

Fade out.   Am I your project

Scene Six

Early morning. AMPARO *and* DOLORES *come out of the house, wearing work clothes.* DOLORES *carries a small bucket of plaster and a trowel.* AMPARO *carries a shovel and heavy gloves.*

DOLORES: This house is falling apart. ¡Ayúdanos, Dios!

AMPARO: You think God is gointu take care of it? Working is what changes things, not oraciones.

DOLORES: Ya te dije, I'm not going to your protesta.

AMPARO *puts on the gloves, begins digging into the yard.* DOLORES *goes over to the side of the house and starts applying plaster to it.*

AMPARO: ¿Sabes qué? I don' even go to church no more, ni recibir comunión . . . coz I'm tire of swallowing what they want to shove down my throat. Body of Christ . . . pedo.

DOLORES: I hate when you talk like this. It makes me sick to my stomach.

AMPARO (*digging more vigorously*): Pues, the truth aint so purty sometimes.

DOLORES: I'm not going. (*To herself:*) You'd think I could get the only son I got to do this for me, pero no. He's always gallivanting around con sus secretos.

AMPARO (*hitting upon something on the ground*): Mira. Hay algo aquí. Ayúdame.

DOLORES: Wha' chu find?

AMPARO: No sé. Help me.

They both get down on their hands and knees and dig. They pull out an old, thick rubber hose.

DOLORES: No es nada.

AMPARO: You don' believe me, but they bury all their poison under our houses. Wha' chu think that crack comes from? An earthquake? The house is sinking, te digo como quicksand.

DOLORES: It's the only house I got.

AMPARO: They lied to us, Lola. They thought we was too stupid to know the difernce. They throw some dirt over a dump, put some casas de cartón on top of it y dicen que it's the "American Dream." Pues, this dream has turned to pesadilla.

DOLORES: Where we apose to go? Every three houses got a For Sale sign. Nobody's gointu buy from us now.

AMPARO: The gov'ment owes us the money.

DOLORES: Oh sí, and they're gointu drop it de los cielos. (*She sits on the porch step.*)

AMPARO: No, pero not'ing gointu change if you don' do not'ing. How can you jus' sit with your hands folded? You see Yolie's baby, ya 'stá malita.

DOLORES: She got a little rash, nomás. Anyway, I do somet'ing before and what good did it do me? Somos mas pobres que antes. A'least before I open my big mouth, Cerezita had a father.

AMPARO: What kina father? A father who wouldn' let his own child feel the sun on her face, who kept her hidden como algo cochino. And now you do the same thing to her. It's not right, Lola. You think hiding her is gointu bring Arturo back?

DOLORES: No. (*Pause.*) It wasn' fair what I did to him. I humiliate him.

AMPARO: Tha's an old tune, comadre. He never humiliate you?

DOLORES: The men are weaker. They can't take what a woman takes.

AMPARO: Adió. You did it to educate the peepo.

DOLORES: I did it to make him ashame. I tole him, "¿Ves? Half a father make half a baby." (*Pause.*) He believe it.

AMPARO: That was a long time ago. Wha' chu got to stop you now?

DOLORES (*returning to plastering*): Vete. Go to your marcha. No tiene nada que ver eso conmigo.

DOLORES *slaps some more plaster onto the wall.* AMPARO *tosses the hose into the junk heap and exits. The sound of a low-flying crop duster fills the stage.* DOLORES *stares up at it as its shadow passes over her. Fade out.*

Scene Seven

The wheels to CERE's *raite can be heard in the darkness. At rise,* MARIO *is on his back, tightening a bolt under the wheelchair.* CEREZITA *is reading a medical book, periodically turning the pages with her mouth. The infant sleeps in her crib.*

CEREZITA: So, what kind of cancer did Memo have?

MARIO: He had a neuroblastoma. Hand me that screwdriver, will you, Cere? (*She picks it up with her mouth, drops it down to him.*) Watch it. You almost hit me.

CEREZITA: I can't see you from up here.

MARIO: Pues, wátchale. (*He rolls the raite back and forth, it squeaks loudly.*) How's that feel?

CEREZITA: Fine, but can you do something about the squeak?

MARIO: Where's the oil?

CEREZITA: Check under the sink. (*He does.*) What's a neuroblastoma?

MARIO (*coming back with the oil*): A tumor. They usually arise in the adrenal gland or any place in the sympathetic chain. (*Pointing out a reference in the book.*) See.

CEREZITA: Like in the chest.

MARIO: Well, they can appear there. Memo's started in the abdomen.

CEREZITA: It says that the prognosis is worse than most leukemia.

MARIO (*applying the oil*): Usually even surgery can't cure it. (*He puts her chin piece back in place.* CEREZITA *gives the raite a little test drive.*) There, a smooth ride. Memo didn't have a chance, Cere. Kids' bodies are so vulnerable. They pick up stuff way before adults. They got no buffer zone. "The canary in the mine shaft" . . . that's exactly what they are. (*He puts the tools away, washes his hands, then runs a comb through his hair.*)

CEREZITA: You going out, Mario?

MARIO: Yeah.

CEREZITA: Tell me the story about the Mayan god before you go.

MARIO: Ah, Cere, my ride's coming.

CEREZITA: Please, don't go just yet.

MARIO: Okay, but the short version. (*Sitting down next to her.*) Cousin Freddie—

CEREZITA: Hadn't been in the states too long, maybe a few months and he liked everything American . . .

MARIO (*amused*): I guess even me. God, Freddie was beautiful. Dark. He had cheekbones to die for, like they were sculpted outta some holy Mayan rock. And he had this little twitch in the side of his jaw that would pulse whenever he got excited or upset or something. The party was still going on and I was supposed to be sleeping in the next room. But Nino Gilberto started singing and letting out those famous gritos of his. . . . (*Imitates "los gritos."*) So, no way, man, was I gonna get any sleep. I could hear Freddie laughing in the patio and I started following his voice around. I'd think about his smile, I'd imagine him waving his hands in people's faces while he talked, getting a little pálido from all the pisto. The next thing I know he's standing—

CEREZITA: No, you forgot the boleros.

MARIO: Right. When the boleros came on, I could hear him singing along with them and I'd think about those veined hands around Yolie's back while they danced, wishing I was there inside those hands. The next thing I know, my young god is standing at the foot of my bed. His shirt's open to his waist . . . more Mayan rock. It's kinda sticking to him from the sweat he's worked up on the dance floor. My little heart is pounding as he tells me how he just came in to check on me. "Mijo," he calls me.

CEREZITA: Mijo.

MARIO: That little twitch pulsing. (*A car horn sounds from the street. He gives* CEREZITA *a peck on the cheek.*) That's it.

CEREZITA: Ah, Mario.

MARIO (*spotting* YOLANDA *through the window*): Look-it, Yolie's coming home. Have her take you out back. It's nice out right now. Ay te watcho. (*He grabs a leather jacket, goes out the door.*)

YOLANDA: Your "friend" is waiting for you, ése. (MARIO *gives her a kiss and exits;* YOLANDA *comes indoors.*) That was one sleazy-looking gringo in that car.

CEREZITA: Mario doesn't like him.

YOLANDA: Well, for not liking him, he sure sees him a lot.

CEREZITA: He gives him things.

YOLANDA: That I believe.

CEREZITA: Take me outside, Yolie.

YOLANDA (*checking the baby in its crib*): Did Lina wake up?

CEREZITA: No. Take me outside, Yolie. Mom's gonna be home soon.

YOLANDA: Okay, let's go. Your hair's lookin' raggedy. I'm gonna give you a good conditioning later. (*Pushing the raite.*) Hey! What happened to the squeak?

CEREZITA (*with pride*): Mario fixed it.

Fade out.

Scene Eight

That evening. CEREZITA *is reading a book.* YOLANDA *passes by with a diaper over her shoulder and a small stack of them in her hands.*

CEREZITA: It recommends making a tea from flor de muerto. It's good for indigestion.

YOLANDA: I'm not giving my baby anything called "flower of the dead."

CEREZITA: It worked for the Aztecs. Zempasuchitl, the yellow marigold.

YOLANDA: Forget it.

YOLANDA *exits.* CEREZITA *shuts the book just as she spots* JUAN *coming up the front steps.*

CEREZITA: Come in.

JUAN (*entering*): Hello. You alone?

CEREZITA: No, Yolie's in back with the baby. Lina's been throwing up her milk.

JUAN: Oh.

CEREZITA: If you came to see my mom, she's next door.

JUAN: No. I came to see you.

CEREZITA: She's trying to get Don Gilberto to stop Amparo from leading the protest at the school tomorrow. Can you hear them?

JUAN: No.

CEREZITA: Sure, my mom's going, "What kina man are you, you can't control your own wife?" And Don Gilberto answers, "I don't gotta control her, I love her."

JUAN: I can't hear them.

CEREZITA: Yeah, but that's what they're saying. Are you going to the demonstration, Father?

JUAN: Yes. I was hoping your mother would bring you.

CEREZITA: No, I don't go out.

JUAN: Never?

CEREZITA: Never. (*She observes* JUAN *for a moment.*)

JUAN: I . . .

CEREZITA: Touch my hair, Father.

JUAN: What?

CEREZITA: Touch my hair. (*He hesitates.*) Go 'head. It's not gonna hurt you. I'm normal from the neck up. (*He touches a strand very gingerly.*)

CEREZITA: Well?

JUAN: It's very . . . smooth.

CEREZITA: Like silk, huh?

JUAN: Yes.

CEREZITA: Oughtabe. Yolie just gave it the works. She studies all these beauty magazines and tries out every new item that hits the market. She's into "natural" these days, which I'm very grateful for. Over the last five years, Yolie experimented in every fashion from beehives to buzzcuts. It was fun for a while, until my hair started falling out. And if my hair doesn't look decent, I don't have much going for me now, do I, Father?

JUAN (*pause*): No, I guess . . . not.

CEREZITA: So now my hair tends to smell more like an overripe tropical garden than anything else. You know, coconut and mango juice shampoo, avocado conditioners, et cetera.

JUAN: I wouldn't know.

CEREZITA: Now it just grows long and thick like a beautiful dark curtain. Nice huh?

JUAN (*touching it again*): Yes.

CEREZITA: I like it, too . . . sometimes just spin my head around and around so I can feel it brush past my cheeks. I imagine it's what those Arab women with the veils must feel like . . . all those soft cloths secretly caressing their bodies.

JUAN: You think about that?

CEREZITA: What, the Arab women? Give me a break, Padre. All I've got is this imagination.

JUAN: Yes . . .

CEREZITA: And a tongue.

JUAN: A tongue?

CEREZITA: Yeah, and mine's got the best definition I bet in the world, unless there's some other vegetable heads like me who survived this valley. Think about it, Padre. Imagine if your tongue and teeth and chin had to do the job of your hands . . . you know, (*She demonstrates.*) turning pages, picking up stuff, scratching an itch, pointing. I mean your tongue alone would have to have some very serious definition. For me . . . well, it's my most faithful organ. Look it up. (*She sticks out her tongue, "pointing" to the dictionary on the   shelf.*)

JUAN: What?

CEREZITA: Get the dictionary. (*Pointing.*) Look up the word *tongue.*

JUAN: But why?

CEREZITA: You'll see. Check it out. (JUAN *gets the dictionary.*)

JUAN (*reading*): "Ton. Tonality. Tone. Tongue. Latin: Lingua."

CEREZITA: Spanish: Lengua.

JUAN: "1 a: a fleshy movable process of the floor of the mouths of most vertebrates that bears sensory end organs and functions especially in taking and swallowing food."

CEREZITA (*reciting from memory*): "2: The power of communication through speech." Your turn, Padre. (*He hesitates.*) Go on.

JUAN: "3: The flesh of the tongue used as food."

CEREZITA (*with* JUAN): "4 a: Language, especially a spoken language."

JUAN: "b: ecstatic usually unintelligible utterance accompanying religious excitation. c: the charismatic gift—"

CEREZITA (*overlapping*): "Of ecstatic speech."

JUAN: The gift of tongues!

CEREZITA: "d: the cry of a hound in sight of game—used especially in the phrase," italicized . . . (*Suggestively.*) "to give tongue." (*She pants like the hound.*)

JUAN: C'mon, now.

CEREZITA: Be a sport, Padre.

JUAN: "Verb. 1 *archaic*: scold."

CEREZITA: "2: to touch or lick with; to project in a tongue."

JUAN: "3: to articulate," parenthetically, "notes by" . . . (*He hesitates.*)

CEREZITA: Yes? . . .

JUAN: "By tonguing."

CEREZITA: My brother Mario brought me a trumpet once, the old medieval kind. No fingering needed . . . just a good, strong tongue. "Tongue in cheek."

JUAN: "Characterized by insincerity, irony, or whimsical exaggeration."

CEREZITA (*provocatively*): "Tongue-lash."

JUAN: "To chide or—"

CEREZITA: Regañar.

JUAN: "Tongueless."

CEREZITA: "Lacking the power of speech."

JUAN: "Mute. Tongue-tied—disinclined or" . . . (*He looks up at her.*)

CEREZITA: "Unable to speak freely."

Fade out.

Scene Nine

The school grounds. McLaughlin Elementary. BONNIE enters carrying a lunch box. DON GILBERTO is pushing a broom. He wears a janitor's uniform which reads McLaughlin School District on back. BONNIE sits, opens her lunch box and takes out an apple. She watches him sweep for a moment.

BONNIE: Don Gilberto, I dreamed Memo before he died.

DON GILBERTO: You did?

BONNIE: Yeah. I dreamed Memo alive playing on the merry-go-round like we used to before he got sick. He's in the middle of it, holding on real tight and I'm pushing the merry-go-round faster and faster. And then I see his face starts to get scared, so I try to stop the merry-go-round but I can't. I can't grab the bars. They just keep hitting my hands harder and harder and he's spinning around so fast that finally his face just turns into a blur. And then he disappears.

DON GILBERTO: Just like that?

BONNIE: Well, then I woke up. (*Pause.*) Now when I go to sleep, I make a prayer so I don't dream about nobody.

DON GILBERTO: What kind of prayer?

BONNIE: Just one that asks God that . . . when I'm sleeping, that he'll keep all the kids outta me. Maybe you make your dreams come true. Maybe you kill people that way.

DON GILBERTO (*taking out a handkerchief from his back pocket and polishing the apple*): Sometimes when you're worried or scared about something, hija, your dreams draw pictures in your sleep to show you what the feelings look like.

BONNIE: Like Memo blurring?

DON GILBERTO: Sí. (*He hands her back the polished apple.*)

BONNIE: I have to think about that, Don Gilberto.

DON GILBERTO: That's all right. You think about it. (*He kisses the top of her head, goes back to sweeping.*)

BONNIE: Look, Don Gilberto! It's the news lady!

ANA PEREZ *appears in front of the "cameras." AMPARO and a group of* PROTESTORS *are approaching, including* MARIO, JUAN, *and* YOLANDA. *They are carrying placards reading, The School Board Lies! Save Our Children! Sin Agua No Tenemos Vida, etc. ANA PEREZ straightens her jacket, lightly brushes back her hair. She addresses the "camera."*

ANA PEREZ: A crowd is beginning to form out here in front of the town of McLaughlin's elementary school. Mostly mothers and other neighbors have shown up this morning. There is no sign of school officials as of yet. Local residents are outraged by the school board's decision to refuse Arrowhead's offer of free drinking water for the schoolchildren. They believe local tap water, contaminated by pesticides, to be the chief cause of the high incidence of cancer among children in the area. They claim that the extensive spraying, especially aerial spraying, causes the toxic chemicals to seep into the public water system. The majority of residents are from a nearby housing tract of federally subsidized housing. It has been alleged that the housing was built on what was once a dump site for pesticides with the full knowledge of contractors. What we have here, Jack, appears to be a kind of 1980s Hispanic Love Canal.

The PROTESTORS *have arrived at the school grounds, led by* DOÑA AMPARO.

DON GILBERTO (*with affection*): She's gonna get me fired, mi vieja.

AMPARO (*under her breath, to* DON GILBERTO): I think I got the cold feet, Berto.

DON GILBERTO: Pues, warm 'em up quick. You got all this gente here esperándote. (*She hesitates.*) ¡Adelante, mujer!

ANA PEREZ: It looks like a local resident will be addressing the crowd.

DON GILBERTO *helps* AMPARO *up onto a bench. The crowd goes quiet. As the speech progresses, the* PROTESTORS *become more and more receptive, calling out in response.*

AMPARO (*tentatively*): Our homes are no longer our homes. They have become prisons. When the water that pours from the sink gots to be boiled three times before it can pass your children's lips, what good is the faucet, the indoor plumbing, the toilet that flushes pink with disease? (*Gaining confidence.*) We were better off when our padres hang some blankets from a tree and we slept under the pertection de las estrellas, because our roofs don' pertect us. A'least then, even if you had to dig a hole in the ground to do your biznis and wipe yourself with newspaper, you could still look up hasta los cielos and see God. But where is God now, amigos? ¿Y el diablo? El diablo hides between the pages of the papeles we sign that makes us afraid. The papeles they have no weight. ¡Ay! They could fly away en la brisa, they could burn hasta una ceniza with a simple household mecha. But our children are flesh and bone. They weigh mucho. You put them all together and they make hunerds and hunerds a pounds of Razita. (*Pause.*) Yesterday, the school board refuse the gift of clean water for our chil'ren's already poisoned throats. The board says, No, there's not'ing wrong with our water. We don' know for sure, it hasn' been prove. How much prove you need? How many babies' bodies pile all up on top of each other in the grave? (*Pause, coming downstage.*) Comadres, compadres. ¿Qué significa que the three things in life—el aire, el agua, y la tierra—que we always had enough of, even in our pueblitos en México, ya no tenemos? Sí, parece que tenemos all that we need. In the morning the air is cool y fresco, the ground stretches for miles, and all that the ranchero puts into it grows big and bright and the water pours from our faucets sin término. Pero, todo es mentira. Look into your children's faces. They tell you the truth. They are our future. Pero no tendremos ningún futuro si seguimos siendo víctimas.

The PROTESTORS *come down into the audience, passing out pamphlets of information about the pesticide problem.* CEREZITA *has been looking out the window at the demonstration.* DOLORES *is sweeping, trying to ignore the sounds of the protest invading her house.*

CEREZITA: Mira, 'amá. They're all going house to house, giving out pamphlets. Father Juanito's there and Don Gilberto. They even got the news cameras.

DOLORES: Get your face out of the window.

CEREZITA: Nobody's looking over here.

DOLORES: Quítate de allí, te digo.

DOLORES *disengages* CEREZITA's *raite and moves her away from the window.*

CEREZITA: Ah, 'amá!

DOLORES: Pues, you don't know who could be out there. All this protesta is bringing the guns down from the sky.

CEREZITA: I just wanted to see.

DOLORES: You don't need to see. (*She gets down on her hands and knees and begins picking up various books and newspapers that* CEREZITA *has left around the floor.*) Mira todos los libros que tienes. One a these days your brain's gointu explode por tantas palabras.

CEREZITA: Wha' else am I supposed to do?

DOLORES: You're suppose to do nothing. I'm suppose to do everything.

CEREZITA: Martyrs don't survive, 'amá.

DOLORES: Your brother teaches you tha' kina talk. Don' get smart with me.

CEREZITA: I am smart.

DOLORES: Maybe you read a lot, but tha' doesn' mean you know about life. You think you find life in a book?

CEREZITA: No, I don't think I find life in a book. (CERE *tosses her hair around, trying to feel it against her cheeks.*)

DOLORES: It's a pig's pen around here, you leave all your junk laying around . . . candy wrappers, the little crumbs from the erasers. (*On her hands and knees, picking at the rug.*) What do you do with them? Chew them?

CEREZITA: Erase.

DOLORES: Mentirosa. I seen you chew them.

CEREZITA: Well, sometimes . . . when I'm thinking.

DOLORES: Well, stop it. It makes a big mess. I can' get those tiny pieces out of l'alfombra. (CEREZITA *lays her face down on the raite, rubs it back and forth, trying to feel her hair against her face.* DOLORES *finds an open book on the floor.*) ¿Qué's esto? Cere?

CEREZITA: Huh? . . . Nothing. It's just one of Mario's old anatomy books.

DOLORES: Es cochino. Tha's what it is? I thought he give you the books to study about the sick peepo. This is not the sick peepo.

CEREZITA: God, Mom, it's just the body.

DOLORES: So, what biznis you got with the body? This jus' puts thoughts in your head. (*She flips through the book.*) ¿Qué tiene que ver una señorita con this kind of pictures? (*Slams it shut.*) I should call in the father.

CEREZITA: Father Juan?

DOLORES: Jus' cuz you don' got a body doesn' mean you can't sin. The biggest sins are in the mind.

CEREZITA: Oh God.

DOLORES: Tu eres una inocente. That's how God wanted it. There's a reason he made you like this. You're old enough now . . .

CEREZITA: I'm old enough now to go out!

DOLORES: Pues vete. (*She engages* CEREZITA's *wheels, puts the chin piece in place.*) You think you're so tough, go on. But we'll see how you feel the first time some stranger looks at you with cruel eyes.

DOLORES *goes to the table. After a pause,* CEREZITA *crosses to her.*

CEREZITA: Give me a chance, 'amá. If nobody ever sees me, how will I know how I look? How will I know if I scare them or make them mad or . . . move them? If people could see me, 'amá, things would change.

DOLORES: No, hija. Dios es mi testigo. I'll never let nobody look at my baby that way.

DOLORES *caresses her.* CERE's *face is rigid as the lights crossfade to* MARIO *and* JUAN *sitting on a park bench.*

JUAN: Why didn't you bring Cerezita out to this?

MARIO: My mom. She protects her.

JUAN: From what?

MARIO: Ridicule. The world.

JUAN: She wanted to be here.

MARIO: You bring her out, then. Maybe Lola would let you. You're God on earth, after all. You're all the protection she'd ever need.

JUAN: She needs you.

MARIO: Oh, Padre, they all need me, but I got other plans.

JUAN: Like what?

MARIO: Getting out. Finishing school. Having a life. One life, not two.

JUAN: Two?

MARIO: You don't know what it's like growing up in this valley.

JUAN: I was born in Sanger, Mario.

MARIO: Yeah? Don't show.

JUAN: My family left when I was about twelve.

MARIO: To LA, right?

JUAN: Right.

MARIO: At least you got out. (*Pause.*) When I was in high school, I used to sit out there in those fields, smoking, watching the cars go by on 99. I'd think about the driver, having somewhere to go. His foot pressed to the floorboard, cruisin'. He was always a gringo. And he'd have one arm draped over the steering wheel and the other around the back of the seat and it'd never occur to him that anybody lived there between those big checkerboard plots of tomatoes, strawberries, artichokes, brussels sprouts, and . . .

JUAN: Grapes.

MARIO: Hundreds of miles of grapes. He'd be headed home to his woman and TV set and sleeping kids tucked into clean sheets and he'd have a wad of bills in his pocket and he'd think he'd live forever. But I'm twenty-five and stuck here in this valley and I know I won't.

JUAN: But twenty-five's so young, Mario.

MARIO: I get high, Padre. I smoke and snort and suck up anything and anyone that will have me. Those are the facts. (*A car horn sounds from the street. MARIO jumps to his feet. He motions to the driver.*) Why did you come back, Father? All you'd need is a nice Buick, a full tank of gas and you'd be indistinguishable on that highway. Just don't stop to pick me up. Your type can destroy me.

MARIO *runs off.* JUAN *watches the car drive away. The lights fade to black.*

Scene Ten

JUAN *fills up a glass of water from the dispenser.*

JUAN: Some of the union people were at the rally. They were trying to enlist people to join in the fast with them. I agreed.

CEREZITA: That's good. People like to see priests and celebrities sacrificing. I'd do it, too, if anyone would notice me. The trick is to be noticed.

JUAN: Six months ago, that's the very thing that brought me here . . . to the Valley.

CEREZITA: What?

JUAN: The union's fast. I saw this newspaper photo of Cesar Chávez. He had just finished a thirty-three-day fast. He looked like a damn saint, a veritable Ghandi. Even the number was holy. Thirty-three.

CEREZITA: The age of Christ's death.

JUAN: So I came home. I came home to the valley that gave birth to me. Maybe as a priest it's vanity to believe you can have a home. The whole church is supposed to be your family, your community, but I can't pretend I don't get lonely.

CEREZITA: Why did you become a priest, Father Juan?

JUAN: Too many years as an altar boy. (*He takes a drink of water.*) And because of the fabric.

CEREZITA: The fabric?

JUAN: Yes. Literally, the cloth itself drew me to be a "man of the cloth." The vestments, the priest's body asleep underneath that cloth, the heavy weight of it tranquilizing him.

CEREZITA: Will you always be a priest, Father Juan?

JUAN: Yes. There's no choice in the matter. Once ordained, you've given up volition in that sense. The priesthood is an indelible mark. You are bruised by it, not violently, but its presence is always felt. A slow dull ache, a slight discoloration in the skin . . .

CEREZITA: A purple-red spot between the eyes, the size of a small stone.

JUAN: I wish I had a third eye, Cere.

CEREZITA: But that's your job, isn't it, Father, to make people see? The 'theology of liberation.' It's a beautiful term. The spiritual practice of freedom. On earth. Do you practice what you preach, Father?

JUAN: It's the people that are to be liberated, not the priests. We're still caught in the Middle Ages somewhere, battling our internal doubts Spanish Inquisition–style. (*Pause.*) I always wanted that kind of six-teenth-century martyr's death. To die nobly and misunderstood, to be exonerated centuries later by a world that was finally ready for me.

CEREZITA (*smiling*): You've been reading too much Lorca.

JUAN: He's my hero.

Fade out.

Scene Eleven

AMPARO *and* DOLORES *return home from work, wearing white uniforms. They are a little tipsy, having stopped off at the local bar for a few beers first. They are singing a ranchera. They come into the house and pull out a few chairs onto the porch.* BONNIE *rides up on a bicycle. Nueva canción music can be heard coming from the radio indoors.*

AMPARO: I dunno how much longer I could aguantar working in tha' place anyway. I dunno wha's worser, the bending to pick en los files or standing on your feet all day in the same damn spot. Me 'stoy poniendo vieja. (*They sit down in front of the house, take off their shoes.*) Mira los bunions. (BONNIE *joins them,* AMPARO *shows her her feet.*) You see how the toes all bunch up there on top of each other? . . . Mi viejo usetu tell me I had beautiful feet. Beautiful. Like a movie star. Ya no.

BONNIE: You want me to rub 'em, Doña Amparo?

AMPARO: ¿Qué, mija?

BONNIE: Your feet. You want me to rub 'em for you?

AMPARO: Pues, okay!

DOLORES: ¡Ay! The royal treatment. (BONNIE *massages* AMPARO's *feet.*)

AMPARO: Your feet get crooked when you gottu squeeze 'em into zapatos que take all the blood from you. They don' tell you cuando eras una chamaca tha' you suffer the rest a your life for the chooz you wear at sixteen. ¿Qué no?

DOLORES: Tha's for darn chure.

AMPARO: Tha's nice, hija. La verdad es que siempre he sido pura ranchera. If I had my way, I'd go barefoot. Ahora these patas don' fit into not'ing but the tenny shoes.

DOLORES (*rolling down her stockings*): What I got is the varicose venas. It's from the cement floors. They squeeze you from the soles up and then el cansancio press you from the neck down. In between, your venas jus' pop out.

BONNIE: Ouch!

AMPARO: Pinche jale. Who needs it?

YOLANDA *comes out onto the porch. She wears rubber gloves, stained with black hair dye.*

YOLANDA: I thought I heard you out here.

DOLORES: You got a custmer, mija?

YOLANDA: Señora Reyes. She's under the dryer.

AMPARO: What color she want this time?

YOLANDA: Midnight blue.

AMPARO: Ya no quiere ser güera.

YOLANDA: I think she's given up . . . tired of fighting the roots.

DOLORES: Bonnie, go get us a coupla beers from the refrigerador, eh?

BONNIE: Okay, Doña Lola. (*She goes to get the beer.*)

DOLORES: ¿Quieres una, mija?

YOLANDA: No. Looks like you two have already had a few.

DOLORES: Una, nomás.

AMPARO: 'Stamos celebrando.

YOLANDA: What?

DOLORES: The varicose venas y los bunions.

AMPARO: They kicked me from the job, hija.

> DOLORES *getures to* YOLANDA *not to ask.*

YOLANDA: But . . . why?

AMPARO: They heard about the protesta. It affect "the workers' morale," me dijeron, que I set a bad example.

YOLANDA: They fired you for speaking at a rally?

AMPARO: Pues, también I was giving out los panfletos from the union.

DOLORES: I tole her not to.

YOLANDA: I can't believe they fired you.

AMPARO: Good thing I got the green card or right now I be on the bus back to Coahuila.

> BONNIE *comes out with the beers, passes them to* DOLORES *and* AMPARO.

DOLORES: Gracias, mija.

BONNIE: Here you go, Doña Amparo.

AMPARO: Thank you, chula.

> *The radio music is suddenly interrupted by a news break.*

RADIO VOICE: This is KKCF in Fresno. News brief. San Salvador. UPI reports that at 6 A.M. this morning six Jesuit priests, along with their housekeeper and her daughter, were found brutally murdered. The priests, from the Central American University, were outspoken opponents to the ruling rightist ARENA party.

DOLORES: Cere! ¡Baja la radio! (*To the women:*) We got enough bad news today without hearing about the rest a the world también. (*The volume lowers, then fades out.*) If she can't be in the world, she brings it into the house and we all gottu know about it. First, it's her brother and now it's the priest. He got her all metida en cosas she got no biznis knowing about.

AMPARO: How long you think you can shelter her from the suffering of the world, Lola? (DOLORES *doesn't respond, puts her shoes back on.*)

DOLORES (*to* YOLANDA): Did your brother come home?

YOLANDA: No. What're you gonna do now without a job, Doña Amparo?

AMPARO: Pues, first thing I put that husband of mine on a diet. (DO-LORES *gets up, looks down the street.*) He still got a job, mija. We'll make it all right. But if they wannu shut me up, they thinking of a purty good way to do it.

DOLORES (*to* YOLANDA): Did he call?

YOLANDA: Who?

DOLORES: Tu hermano.

YOLANDA: Yeah, he said he's leaving on Saturday. He's already packed, 'amá.

DOLORES: Fine. I'm tired of worrying for him. This way, if you don' know nothing, you got nothing to worry about.

YOLANDA: He said if you wanted he'd come by Friday night.

DOLORES: Díle que no thank you. I don' wan' no good-byes. I had enough good-byes already in my life.

AMPARO: Pues, you tell mi querido ahijado he better not move nowhere without saying good-bye to his padrinos. It would break his Nino's heart.

YOLANDA: I'll tell him, Doña Amparo.

YOLANDA *goes back inside to check on Señora Reyes. Crossfade to* JUAN, *who is walking to the Valle home, books stuffed under one arm. He reads from a newspaper article.*

JUAN: They blasted their brains out in their sleep! Just like that!

DON GILBERTO *enters carrying a lunch pail, returning home from work.*

DON GILBERTO: ¿Qué le pasa, Padre? It looks like you saw one of those holy ghosts of yours.

JUAN: 'Scuze me?

DON GILBERTO: Read some bad news, Father?

JUAN: Yes. (*He shows* DON GILBERTO *the article.*)

DON GILBERTO: Did you know the guys?

JUAN: No, but they were Jesuits, my order.

DON GILBERTO: You'd think a priest in a Catholic country couldn't get shot up in his pajamas.

JUAN: But they were intellectuals.

DON GILBERTO: That didn't seem to matter too much to the bullets, Padre.

DON GILBERTO pats JUAN on the shoulder, continues on home. YO-LANDA comes out onto the porch.

DOLORES: ¿Y la Señora Reyes?

YOLANDA: She fell asleep under the dryer.

AMPARO: I hope she like el cabello frito.

BONNIE: Fried hair?

AMPARO: Un estilo nuevo, mija.

The laughter of the women calls JUAN's attention. He crosses to them.

DOLORES: Oh, hello, Father.

JUAN: Buenas tardes.

YOLANDA: Visiting the sick again, Padre?

JUAN: No. Yes . . . I mean I have some books for Cerezita. (*To* DOLORES:) If that's all right with you, señora?

DOLORES: Go 'head. What else she gottu do, la pobre. (*He starts to go inside.*) Oh, Father . . . (*He stops at the door.*) Can you come over to the house Friday night? Mi hijo is moving to San Francisco and we gointu have a little get-together, nothing fancy, just some enchiladas rojas. Son Mario's fav'rit.

JUAN: Of course, I'd love to. . . . ¿Con su permiso?

DOLORES: Pásale. Pásale. (*He goes inside. To* AMPARO:) And bring tu viejo. This way he gets some food in his estómago antes que you start to starve him to death.

YOLANDA: ¡Orale! ¡Una pachanga!

DOLORES: I dint say nothing about una pachanga.

YOLANDA: You know what happens when Don Gilberto comes—it's party time!

DOLORES: Pues, it'll be nice to have some men in the house for a change.

AMPARO: And tha' priest, he's plenty a man.

YOLANDA: Yeah, I don't trust him.

DOLORES: He means well, hija.

AMPARO: Pero you know wha' they say, Lola. A man is a man first, no matter wha' he is. If he's a priest or an uncle or a brother, no importa.

THE WOMEN (*to* BONNIE): ¡Un hombre es un hombre!

They laugh. The lights fade out.

Scene Twelve

Música Norteña. At rise, a pachanga in full swing. The records are spinning, the beer and tequila are flowing. JUAN sits at the kitchen table watching MARIO and AMPARO dance. CEREZITA is just finishing a game of Lotería with BONNIE. DON GILBERTO is playing la guitarra, while DOLORES sits on the couch, embroidering a dishcloth. YOLANDA sits next to her, holding the baby. After a few minutes, DON GILBERTO, who's pretty well plastered, puts his guitar down and pours himself another beer.

DON GILBERTO: ¿Sabe qué, Padre? I love that muchacho. He's lo máximo. You wanna know the truth, Padre? That boy's not just my godson, he's my real son. That's right, mi propio hijo cuz I love him that much. Right, hijo?

MARIO: That's right, Nino.

DON GILBERTO: An' he's getting outta this pinche valle.

DOLORES: Compadre!

DON GILBERTO: I can talk like that with you. ¿No, Padre? You're off duty right now.

JUAN: Sure you can.

DON GILBERTO: That's right. God's back there in the church. The only men we got at this table are hombres de carne y hueso. Vieja!

AMPARO: ¿Qué?

DOLORES (*intervening*): Wha' chu handsome men wan' here?

DON GILBERTO: Tenemos sed, comadre.

DOLORES: Coming right up.

AMPARO helps DOLORES with the drinks, preparing the tequila, salt and lemon. They take a few shots themselves. MARIO joins the men at the table.

DON GILBERTO: She's got a heart of gold, that woman. And she loves her kids ¿sabe? There aint nothin' she wouldn't do for her kids. Look-it Cerezita over there. (CEREZITA *is radiant.*) 'Sta contenta because she knows she got a family, a mother, that loves her. It's hard, Padre. . . . You listenin' to me, Padre?

JUAN (*pulling his gaze from* CEREZITA): . . . Yes.

DON GILBERTO: You can imagine how hard it's been for Dolores, but she did it, and alone. My compadre . . . bueno, it's hard to even call him that now after leaving his family like he did. When a man leaves his wife alone to raise his kids, well to me that no longer qualifies him to be a man. A big macho, maybe. Maybe he can fool las viejas, act like que tiene huevos. But that's the easy part, jumping in and out of the sack. A real man tiene brazos. Nos llaman braceros because we work and love with our arms. Because we aint afraid to lift a sack of potatoes, to defend our children, to put our arms around la waifa at night. This family, they've suffered a lot, Padre. When a father leaves, it's like cutting off the arms of the family. (*Hugging* MARIO.) Even this guy. He had a lot on his shoulders. ¡Chihuahua! I usetu remember this little mocoso coming home from school all the time with his nose all bloody. He wasn' a fighter. But after so many times, finally, Dolores tells me, "Compadre, tienes que hacer algo." (*He brings* MARIO *to his feet, starts to box with him.*) So, I put the gloves on him and showed him my famous "apricot." (DON GILBERTO *winds up, lets out a wild "uppercut" in the air and ends up on his butt. They all rush to him.*) And they never messed with him again. Right, hijo?

MARIO: Right.

DON GILBERTO: ¡Eso!

JUAN: So, all your kids are grown, Don Gilberto?

DON GILBERTO: Well, I guess that's why la vieja and me, we kina adopt these guys. We couldn't have no children. Amparo's a good woman, she wanted kids bad! But it was me. She never tells nobody cuz she thinks I get ashamed. But it's biology, right, Padre? Mi madre, she had two of us, see. And my cuate, well it seems he just hogged up all the jugo, if you know what I mean. He got a pile of kids, nietos too. (*He takes another shot.*) ¿Y tú, Padre? What's your excuse?

JUAN: . . . I'm a priest.

DON GILBERTO: That's no excuse! (*Busting up.*) When los conquistadores come to América with their priests, half the Mexican population got fathers for fathers! (*Busting up again.*)

JUAN (*embarrassed*): I don't know. You just make choices, . . . I guess.

DON GILBERTO: Pues, sometimes you don't get to choose. But that just teaches you que you gotta make familia any way you can.

AMPARO: Ya, viejo. You gointu put the father to sleep con tanta plática. Mira, the father's glass is almost empty.

DON GILBERTO: Pues, fill it up then.

DOLORES: Aquí lo tengo ya. (*She carries a tray with drinks.*)

DON GILBERTO: ¡Tequila! ¡Sí! ¡Celebremos! You watch, mi ahijado's gointu go to the big university. He's gointu be a doctor someday and cure all the sickness que tiene nuestra raza. Right, mijo?

MARIO: That's right, Nino.

DON GILBERTO: Pues, lez drink to that. (*Toasting.*) ¡Salud! (*They all raise their glasses.*)

JUAN: Amor, dinero.

MARIO: Y tiempo para gozarlos.

DON GILBERTO: ¡Eso! (DON GILBERTO *picks up the guitar again and the family joins in singing "Volver."*)

> 'Y volver, volver, volver
> a tus brazos otra vez.
> Llegaré hasta donde 'stés.
> Yo sé perder, yo sé perder.
> Quiero volver, volver, volver.'

MARIO *rises, lights a cigarette, and steps out onto the porch.* DOLORES's *eyes follow him.*

JUAN (*to* DOLORES): May I have this dance?

DOLORES: You don' dance to "Volver," Padre. You cry.

JUAN: May I have this cry?

DOLORES: Bueno, I think this one, pues . . . it's all mine.

Crossfade to MARIO *smoking on the porch. He watches the sky as the fog begins to roll in. Sound of crop duster overhead. He waves back at it sarcastically.* DOLORES *comes out onto the porch.*

DOLORES: Why they spraying at night now?

MARIO: Nobody sees them that way. Nobody that matters anyway.

DOLORES: I'm tired of it. I wish we were all going away.

MARIO: I'm sorry.

DOLORES: Really.

MARIO: Yes.

DOLORES: But it doesn't stop you from leaving us.

MARIO: I want a future, 'amá.

DOLORES: The school is not why you're going. It's something else.

MARIO: What?

DOLORES: You're leaving with a secret.

MARIO: It's no secret, 'amá. You're the only one that doesn't want to see it.

DOLORES: I'm not talking about that. I know already for a long time. You think I dint know since the time you was little? How you want to do everything like Yolie. Play with her dolls, put on her dresses. "Jus' pertend," you say, "jus' pertend, mami." Pertend, nada. Me chocó the first time I seen your hands digging into Yolie's purse like they belong there. (*Grabbing his hands.*) Look at your hands, hijo. Son las manos de tu padre, las manos de un obrero. Why you wannu make yourself como una mujer? Why you wannu do this to the peepo who love you?

MARIO (*pulling his hands away*): Who loves me, 'amá?

DOLORES: Tienes familia.

MARIO: Family you don't take to bed.

DOLORES: You think those men who put their arms around you in the night are gointu be there to take care of you in the morning?

MARIO: No.

DOLORES: Necesitas familia, hijo. What you do fuera del matrimonio is your own biznis. You could have familia. Eres hombre. You don' gottu be alone, not like Yolie. Who's gointu want her con una niña already?

MARIO: I can't do that, 'amá. I can't put my body one place and my heart another. I'm not my father.

DOLORES: He loved us, hijo.

MARIO: He loved his women, too.

DOLORES: Can't you forget that? You hold that in your heart, it's gointu poison you.

MARIO: Can you? We've always been lonely, 'amá. You and me waiting for someone to come along and just talk to us with a little bit of kindness, to tell us how fine and pretty we are, to lie to our face.

DOLORES: Me das asco.

MARIO: Why? Because I remind you of you. What love did you ever get from my dad? He had a sweet mouth, that's all. A syrupy tongue that every time he dragged himself home, could always talk you back into loving him. That's not the kind of man I want to be.

DOLORES: You'd rather suffer like a woman instead?

MARIO: No.

DOLORES: God made you a man and you throw it away. You lower yourself into half a man.

MARIO: I don't want to fight, 'amá. I'm leaving in the morning. Give me your blessing. Send me on my way with the sign of the cross and a mother's love.

DOLORES: No puedo.

MARIO: You don't have to approve of it, 'amá.

DOLORES: No puedo. Peepo like you are dying. They got tha' sickness. How can I give mi bendición para una vida que te va a matar. God makes this sickness to show peepo it's wrong what they do. Díme que te vas a cambiar y te doy mi bendición. Tu eres el único macho. I want you to live.

MARIO: I want to live, too. I can't make you see that. Your god's doing all the seeing for you.

MARIO *takes off down the street.*

Scene Thirteen

The party is over. CEREZITA *is looking out the window.* DON GILBERTO *is asleep in the chair.* AMPARO *and* JUAN *are just finishing the dishes.* YOLANDA *has retired with the baby.* BONNIE *is asleep on the couch.*

CEREZITA: Mario won't return to us. He will grow ill like his brother and we will ignore this brother, this son, this child of ours who failed in his manly destiny.

JUAN *puts the last of the dishes away.*

AMPARO: Gracias, Father. But don't tell Dolores I let you help me. She kill me. ¡Imagínese! A priest doing the dishes!

JUAN: I enjoyed it.

AMPARO: That's coz you don't haftu do it every day. (*She goes over to* BONNIE, *awakens her.*) C'mon, mija. Ya nos vamos.

BONNIE: Okay.

AMPARO: Bueno, I guess I better try to get this old man out of here.

JUAN: You need help?

AMPARO: No, I'm usetu it. (*She goes to* DON GILBERTO *and nudges him awake.*)

DON GILBERTO (*startled*): Soñé contigo, vieja. You had un montón de chamacos mamando tu pecho.

AMPARO (*helping him to his feet*): The only baby I got is right here.

DON GILBERTO: I was so proud!

AMPARO: You tell Dolores I talk to her in the morning.

JUAN: Sure.

AMPARO (*to* CEREZITA): Good night, mija.

CEREZITA: Good night, Doña Amparo . . . Don Gilberto. (DON GIL-BERTO *throws her a kiss.*)

BONNIE: 'Night, Cere.

CEREZITA: 'Night, mija.

They exit. JUAN *comes up behind* CEREZITA. *He stares out the window.*

JUAN: There's nothing to see. The fog's barely a foot from the window.

CEREZITA: Sometimes I wish it would swallow the whole house up. I don't blame Mario for leaving. I'd leave if I could.

JUAN: You're gonna miss him, aren't you?

CEREZITA: There's nothing for him here. No Mayan gods. Nothing.

JUAN (*awkwardly*): Well, I guess I better go, too. Do you . . . need something before I leave?

CEREZITA: Yeah, just put a towel over my cage like the canaries. Martyrs don't survive.

JUAN: Cere, I . . .

CEREZITA: I want out, Father! Out into that street! And I will not have time for anybody who can't help me.

She turns her face away. JUAN *hesitates for a moment, then leaves.*

JUAN (*passing* DOLORES *coming back into the yard*): Buenas noches, señora. Gracias.

DOLORES: Buenas noches, Padre.

JUAN *starts to say more, but she has already started toward the house. He exits. Moments later, the sound of the crop duster passes overhead again.* DOLORES *follows the sound.*

DOLORES: Why don't you just drop a bomb, cabrones! It'd be faster that way!

The lights fade to black.

ACT II

Scene One

Several months later, DOLORES *is sneaking around the outside of the front of the house. Crouching down behind a bush, she peaks into the windows, trying not to be seen.* JUAN *is passing by. He is saying prayers from his breviary, his lips moving silently.*

JUAN (*nearly bumping into her*): Señora Valle.

DOLORES: ¡Ay, Padre! Me asustó.

JUAN: ¿Qué hace, señora?

DOLORES (*conspiratorially*): I'm looking through the windows.

JUAN: But . . . why?

DOLORES: To know, Father.

JUAN: To know what?

DOLORES: To know what you can see inside the house at night. The peepo going by can see through the windows. ¿Qué vió, Padre, when you were coming up the street?

JUAN: No sé. I wasn't paying attention.

DOLORES: Next time, Father, you pay attention, eh? So you can tell me from how far away you can see wha's going on inside the house.

JUAN: Certainly, I . . .

DOLORES: Cere don' wan' the shades down. She wants to look at the street lamps, she say.

JUAN: Es todo lo que tiene, Señora Valle.

DOLORES: Sí, pero anybody que pasa por aquí can see we don' got no men in the house. Mire, Father. (*Indicates the window.* JUAN *crouches down next to her.*) Can you tell Cere is sick from here?

JUAN: What do you mean?

DOLORES: ¡Que no tiene cuerpo!

JUAN: No, no se ve.

DOLORES: It looks like she could just be sentada, no?

JUAN: Sí, sentada or stooping behind something.

DOLORES: Bueno, tha's all I needed to know. Gracias, Padre.

JUAN: Buenas noches.

DOLORES: Buenas noches.

> JUAN *continues on with his prayers,* DOLORES *goes inside.* YOLANDA *sits near the baby's crib.* CEREZITA *is reading.*

YOLANDA: I can't get her to feed. She keeps pulling her face away.

DOLORES: Pues, no tiene hambre.

YOLANDA: Yesterday was the same. Look. She just sleeps. I have to wake her up to feed her.

DOLORES: ¿Tiene calentura?

YOLANDA: A little. I took her temperature about an hour ago.

DOLORES: ¿Y que te dijeron en la clínica?

YOLANDA: Nothing much. They say maybe there's something wrong with my milk. They gave me formula. She doesn't want that either.

DOLORES: A ver . . . (*Goes over to the baby, checks for a temperature.*) Todavía tiene un poco de calentura. Get some cold toallitas y pónselas en la frente. Tal vez that'll bring her fiebre down.

YOLANDA: I'm scared she's really sick, 'amá.

DOLORES: No pienses así. Traele la toallita. (YOLANDA *goes to get the wet cloth, applies it to the baby's forehead.* DOLORES *serves up sopa from the stove for* CERE, *puts a napkin under her chin, begins spooning the food into her mouth.*) Así me rechazabas when you was a baby. All of a sudden, you dint wan' the chichi no more.

CEREZITA: That was a long time ago, 'amá.

DOLORES: But a mother never forgets those things . . . cuando su bebé turns her face away like that.

> *She continues feeding* CEREZITA, *periodically wiping her mouth.* AMPARO *enters carrying a large, rolled-up chart.*

AMPARO: I'm jus' in time for dinner, eh?

DOLORES: Sí, comadre. Ya 'stá caliente la cena.

AMPARO: No, no. I'm just kidding. Ya comí. (*Going to the baby.*) Ahora ¿cómo esta?

YOLANDA: Igual.

AMPARO: I'm sorry, hija. (*Beat.*) Vente. Quiero enseñarles algo.

YOLANDA: ¿Qué?

AMPARO: Hice un mapa. (*She unrolls the chart onto the table.*) A chart of all the houses en la vecindad que tiene gente con the health problems.

YOLANDA: Let me see.

AMPARO: Miren, the red dots mean those houses got someone with cancer. Estos puntos azules donde tienen tumores. Los green ones son para birth defects y los amarillos, the miscarriages.

YOLANDA: What are all these orange dots?

AMPARO: Bueno, smaller problems como problemas del estómago, las ronchas, cosas así.

YOLANDA: Cheezus, it's the whole damn neighborhood.

CEREZITA: Where's our house?

AMPARO: Aquí donde están the orange dot and the green dot.

CEREZITA: That's me, the green dot.

YOLANDA (*lightly*): You put us on the map, Cere.

CEREZITA: That's right. (*They laugh.*)

DOLORES: Go 'head, make the jokes. (*To* AMPARO:) ¿Por qué traes estas cosas a mi casa?

AMPARO: Bueno, I—

DOLORES: I got one baby que eighteen years later I still got to feed and clean and wipe, que no tiene ni la capacidad to put a spoon a food in her mouth. I got a grandchild si no 'stá llorando por las ronchas, she sleeps all day sin ganas de comer, and I got a son que might as well be dead coz almost a year go by and I don' know nothing about him. So, I don' need a chart to tell me que tengo problemas.

AMPARO: I'm not trying to tell you about your problems, comadre. I'm trying to tell you que no 'stás sola.

DOLORES: I am alone and I'm not gointu hold out my hand como una mendiga a nadie.

AMPARO: No one's going begging. It's not begging to make the government pay for what we got coming to us.

YOLANDA: We need help, 'amá.

DOLORES: Vete. Take tu comunismo someplace else.

AMPARO: Ay, Lola, me das vergüenza. Soy tu comadre. Don' make me into a stranger.

DOLORES: Pues ya no te reconozco. You change since they put your picture in the papers and on the TV. I think you like it.

YOLANDA: That's not fair, 'amá.

AMPARO: No, tiene razón tu madre. It does give me somet'ing. It makes me feel good to watch peepo que no tiene ni educación ni sus papeles, show the guts to fight para sus niños.

DOLORES: ¿Qué sabes tú? No tienes niños.

YOLANDA: 'Amá. (*The baby cries.* YOLANDA *starts toward it, but* DOLORES *intercepts.*)

DOLORES: This is my work. (*Patting the infant. The cries subside.*) When you got a baby, when you feel that baby come out entre las piernas, nothing is the same after that. You are chain to that baby. It doesn' matter how old they get or how far away they go, son tus hijos and they always take a piece of you with them. So you walk around full of holes from all the places they take from you. All the times you worry for them—where they are, who they with, what they doing. All the times you see them suffer on their faces and your hands are tied down from helping them. Como se puede sentir una mujer whole and strong como quieres tú with so many empty places in her body? El Dios es el único que nos llena. Not you and not your gov'ment. (*She goes to* AMPARO, *grabs the chart from her.*) This is the las' time I'm gointu say it, I don' wan' this biznis in my house.

DOLORES *throws the chart out the door and goes back to feeding* CEREZITA, *shoving the food into her mouth.* AMPARO *leaves in silence. Fade out.*

Scene Two

Lights rise on front room. CEREZITA *is watching* BONNIE *play. She is constructing a coffin out of a small shoe box.* DOLORES *sits on the sofa, softly murmuring the rosary.*

BONNIE: We knew she wouldn't make it. The cancer got her.

CEREZITA: How did you know?

BONNIE: She bled through all her openings: her mouth, her ears, her nose . . . even through her pee hole, she bled. It was outta control.

CEREZITA: What are you doing now?

BONNIE: I gotta bury her. I'm making her coffin.

CEREZITA: The shoe box is her coffin?

BONNIE: Yeah, but I'm making it real purty inside. I got some valentine cards in there and some of Yolie's ribbon for her hair. See, look. (*She shows* CEREZITA *the box.*)

CEREZITA: Yeah, Rosie will be nice and cozy in there.

YOLANDA *enters with an overnight bag. She stops at the door, riveted by* BONNIE's *words.*

BONNIE: Lina's gonna die, too, just like this. When they send the children to the hospital, they never come back. They keep 'em in the hospital bed until they put 'em in a box. Then they'll put dirt over her face. When she wakes up, she won't be able to breathe cuz the dirt will be in her nose and her mouth. (BONNIE *shows the box to* YOLANDA *as a kind of offering.*) Look, Yolie.

Horrified, YOLANDA *goes into the kitchen, pours herself a shot of tequila and sits at the table.* DOLORES *goes to her.*

DOLORES: I know what you're feeling. I know what it feels like to have a sick baby. When Cerezita come out of me, I dint even wannu look at her, I tole the doctors to put a blanket over her head to suffocate her, but she scream and scream so loud, the doctors couldn' do it. They tole me un grito así means the baby wants to live with all its heart and soul.

YOLANDA: Evalina's dying, 'amá. My baby's dying.

DOLORES: No hables así. You don' know tha'!

YOLANDA: I know it's a tumor. I know it's malignant. I know what that means.

DOLORES: It means you gottu pray to God. Fíjate. Cerezita es un milagro. Every day that she lives, it's prove que el Dios does not forget us.

YOLANDA: He's forgotten you and me and everybody else in this goddamn valley. (*Sound of low-flying helicopter suddenly fills the air. Searchlights flood the kitchen windows.* YOLANDA *rushes to the front door, swings it open, runs outside.*) Take me! You mutherfuckers!

DOLORES (*going after her*): Yolie! No, they'll see you! Mija! (YOLANDA *is ablaze with light. Chopper sounds grow nearer.*)

YOLANDA (*shouting into the sky*): C'mon, you sonavabitches! Take me! C'mon! Here I am! Look-it! Shoot me you mutherfuckers! Kill me!

DOLORES (*grabbing her*): No, mija! Come back in. (DOLORES *and* YO-LANDA *fall to the ground together weeping as the chopper retreats.*)

YOLANDA: Don't you see, 'amá? I gotta find her killer. Put a face to him, a name, track him down and make him suffer the way we suffer. I want to kill him, 'amá. I want to kill some . . . goddamn body!

DOLORES (*stroking her*): Sí, mija. Sí. Ya lo sé, hija. I know.

DOLORES *helps her daughter to her feet and brings her back into the house. The lights fade to black.*

Scene Three

Lights rise to reveal a political demonstration. ANA PEREZ, *in an overcoat and scarf, stands before the "cameras" with a microphone. In the distance, the* PRO-TESTORS *are approaching, the* MOTHERS *wearing white bandanas. Their expressions are heavy with the faces of the dying and the memory of the already dead. The* PROTESTORS *carry signs reading,* Boycott Grapes, No Compre Uvas, *etc. One child holds up a sign saying,* Quiero Vivir! *and another,* I Want to Live! *The red-and-black Union of Campesino flags can be seen above their heads.* DON GILBERTO *and* JUAN *are among the protestors, as are* BONNIE *and the* CHILDREN. *A drum beats slowly.*

ANA PEREZ: It's a frostbitten morning here in Sacramento, Jack, but that hasn't discouraged the Mothers and Friends of McLaughlin from making the long trek up here from their home at the southern-most end of the San Joaquin Valley.

PROTESTORS (*chanting*): '¡El pueblo unido jamás será vencido!' (*They continue to the beat of the drum.*)

ANA PEREZ: The mothers' demands are quite concrete. They believe that the federal government should pay for their families' relocation to an environmentally safe community, since federal moneys subsidized the building of their housing tract. They further demand that the well which provides tap water for the area be shut down and never again be used for drinking water. And finally they urge the governor to see to the establishment of a free health clinic for affected families and to monitor the growing incidence of cancer in the region. (*The* PROTESTORS *begin to move downstage. They stand shoulder to shoulder.*) Amparo Manríquez, the founder of Mothers for McLaughlin, has approached the capitol steps. I understand they have prepared some kind of statement.

As AMPARO *steps forward, she holds up a picture of a dead child. Each of the* MOTHERS *follows in the same manner.*

AMPARO: Sandy Pérez. Died August 15, 1982. Ailment: acute leukemia. Age 9.

MOTHER: Frankie Gonzales. Died March 16, 1986. Ailment: bone cancer. Age 10.

MOTHER: Johnny Rodríguez. Died July 10, 1987. Ailment: adrenal gland tumor. Age 5.

MOTHER: Rosalinda Lorta. Died June 5, 1980. Ailment: chest muscle tumor. Age 5.

MOTHER: Maira Sánchez. Died August 30, 1987. Ailment pituitary tumor. Age 6.

MOTHER: Mario Bravo. Died November 26, 1987. Ailment: cancer of the liver. Age 14.

MOTHER: Memo Delgado. Died October 24, 1988. Ailment: adrenal gland tumor. Age 6.

YOLANDA: Evalina Valle. Died November 2, 1989. Ailment . . . ailment . . . era mi hija . . . era . . . ¡mi hija!

She collapses in AMPARO's *arms. The* PROTESTORS *advance, forming a line of resistance. A* POLICEMAN *in riot gear holds back the crowd. They continue to press forward.*

PROTESTORS: ¡Asesinos! ¡Asesinos! ¡Asesinos! . . .

BONNIE *slips.* AMPARO *steps out of the line to retrieve her. The* POLICEMAN *knocks* AMPARO *down with his nightstick.*

ANA PEREZ: She's been struck! Amparo Manríquez . . . oh my god! The policeman! . . . (*He continues to beat her in slow, methodical blows.*) Stop him! Jesus! Somebody stop him! No! No! Stop him!

DON GILBERTO *breaks through the line and throws his body over* AMPARO *to shield her. The* PROTESTORS *scatter. Black out.*

Scene Four

JUAN *has brought* CEREZITA *outdoors. The sun is setting. Black silhouettes of pecan trees on the horizon, grape vineyards in the foreground.* CEREZITA *is transfixed by the view.* JUAN *paces back and forth nervously.* BONNIE *is on the porch, softly singing a lullaby. She ties two twigs together in the shape of a cross, then hangs her doll onto it, wrapping string around its wrists and ankles.*

BONNIE:

> 'Duerme, duerme, negrito,
> que tu mama está en el campo, negrito.
> Te va a traer rica fruta para tí.
> Te va a traer muchas cosas para tí . . .'

JUAN: I got scared. I don't know why. I . . . I could have done something. They beat her so bad, Cere.

CEREZITA: Heroes and saints.

JUAN: What?

CEREZITA: That's all we can really have for now. That's all people want.

JUAN: They want blood?

> CERE *glances at him, presses her mouth to the raite button, and comes downstage.* JUAN *looks over to* BONNIE. *She waves back with the crucified doll.*

CEREZITA: Look, Juan, it looks like a thousand mini-crucifixions out there.

JUAN: What?

CEREZITA: The vineyards. See all the crosses? It's a regular cemetery. (JUAN *comes up behind her; his eyes scan the horizon.*) The trunk of each of the plants is a little gnarled body of Christ writhing in agony. Don't you see it?

JUAN: Sort of.

CEREZITA: See how the branches look like arms with the bulging veins of suffering. Each arm intertwined with the other little crucified Christs next to it. Thousands of them in neat orderly rows of despair. Syphilitic sacks of grapes hanging from their loins.

JUAN: How do you see these things, Cere?

CEREZITA: I see it all. A chain gang of Mexican Christs. Their grey wintered skin, their feet taking root into the trenches the machines have made.

JUAN: They *are* lifelike, aren't they?

CEREZITA: They're dead. (*Suddenly the sun bursts through a cloud. It bathes* CEREZITA's *face. She basks in it for a moment.*)

> The living dead of winter.
> Dead to the warmth of sun on my face
> melting into the horizon.
> Pecan trees like rigid skeletons
> black against the sky.

Dead to the deep red and maroon
the grapevines bleed.
Dead to the smell of earth,
split moist and open
to embrace the seed.

BONNIE *approaches. She carries two small two-by-fours.*

BONNIE: I got the wood, Cere.

CEREZITA: Bring it here, mija.

JUAN (*stopping her*): No! Give it to me.

BONNIE *hesitates, looks to* CEREZITA.

CEREZITA: Dásela.

BONNIE (*handing the wood over to him*): Are you gonna make the cross, Father Juan?

He raises up the two pieces of wood, forming them into the shape of a small, child-sized cross. His eyes are fixed on CERE's.

JUAN: Yes.

Sudden flute and tambor. Fade out.

Scene Five

The hospital. DON GILBERTO *brings* AMPARO *out in a wheelchair. She has a black eye and wears a hospital gown and carries a small purse on her lap.* JUAN *is with them.* DON GILBERTO *sits, takes out a racing form.*

AMPARO: They cut out my spleen, Father. It was completely smash.

DON GILBERTO: El Doctor Fong . . . es un Chino ¿sabes? He says que the spleen is the part of the body que 'stá conectado con el coraje.

JUAN: It's the place of emotion, of human passions.

AMPARO: Pues, that policia got another thing coming if he think he could take away mi pasión. ¿No, viejo?

DON GILBERTO: Yeah, she already been trying to pull me on top of her in the wheelchair. She gonna bust her stitches I tell her.

AMPARO: No seas exagerado. (*To* JUAN:) The doctor dice que me parezco a su madre, que I'm tough like his mother con el dolor.

DON GILBERTO (*teasing*): Mi Chinita.

AMPARO: Cállete el hocico tú. El padre came to visit me. I'm the sick one. (DON GILBERTO *smiles, starts reading the racing form. As the conversation ensues, he begins to nod off, then finally falls asleep. The newspaper lies draped across his chest.*) Y Dolores . . . ¿cómo 'stá?

JUAN: Yolanda seems to be handling the baby's death better than Señora Valle. I had to pull her out of the bushes last night.

AMPARO: ¿Otra vez?

JUAN: This was worse. It was already past midnight, and she wouldn't budge. She said she had seen Mario's ghost . . .

AMPARO: ¿Cómo?

JUAN: That Mario's ghost was trying to get back into the house.

AMPARO: ¡Qué raro!

JUAN: She was shaking . . . and as white as a ghost herself.

AMPARO: Pero ¿por qué dijo eso?

JUAN: I don't know. Nobody can reach Mario.

AMPARO: My comadre is a very scared woman, Father. (*Pause.*) Mira.

> AMPARO *takes a news clipping out of her purse, unfolds it, hands it to* JUAN.

JUAN: It's Cerezita.

AMPARO: Barely two years old and in *The New York Times*. Fifteen years ago, Cere's face was in all the newspapers, then Dolores just shut up.

JUAN: Why?

AMPARO: She lost her husband on account of it.

JUAN: On account of what?

AMPARO: Advertising his sins. She believe Cere was a sign from God to make her husband change his ways. But he dint change, he left.

JUAN: But it was pesticides.

AMPARO: In her heart, Dolores feels difernt. Nobody wants to be a víctima, Father. Better to believe that it's the will of God than have to face up to the real sinners. They're purty powerful, those sinners. You start to take them on, pues you could lose. This way, por lo menos, you always get to win in heaven. Isn' that what the Church teaches, Father?

JUAN: Well, the Church counsels that—

AMPARO: You gointu do the rosary tonight, Father?

JUAN: Yes. At seven, then the vigil will go on all night.

AMPARO: And Cerezita will be there?

JUAN: Yes, it's at the house.

AMPARO (*looking over to make sure* DON GILBERTO *is asleep*): Cuídala, Father. Don' let her go out tonight.

JUAN: But Cere . . . never goes out.

AMPARO: The men in the helicopters, they're hired by the growers. Anybody out en los files tonight, they'll shoot them. They don' wan' no more publeesty about the crucifixions.

JUAN: Then you think Cere—

AMPARO: I don' think not'ing. I'm jus' asking you not to let your eyes leave her tonight. Hazme el favor.

JUAN: Of . . . course.

AMPARO: Bueno. Now give me one of those priest's prayers of yours. A ver si me ayuda.

JUAN: You want me to pray for you?

AMPARO: Insurance, Padre.

He smiles. AMPARO *closes her eyes as* JUAN *blesses her. The lights fade to black.*

Scene Six

Later that night. CEREZITA *is sleeping.* DOLORES *is standing by the small coffin. It is surrounded by candles and flowers. Trancelike, she takes one of the candles and places it on* CEREZITA's *raite. She kneels before her.*

DOLORES: I can't pray no more to a God no tiene oídos. Where is my Dios, mija? I turn to you coz I got nobody left now. Give me a sign mi querida virgencita. Enséñame como aliviarnos del dolor que nos persigue en este valle de lágrimas.

CEREZITA *slowly opens her eyes, sees her mother praying to her.*

CEREZITA: Go to sleep now, 'amá. I'll watch over Evalina.

DOLORES: Gracias, virgencita. (*She rises, carrying the candle, goes to the window.*) Mario carried death with him. I saw it in his cansancio, in the way his head fell down, tan pesada entre los hombros. In the way he put one foot onto the porch and then the other . . . and then he change his mind. (DOLORES *blows out the candle, as she does the others by the coffin. With each one, she names her progeny.*) I miss my babies, mi Evalina, mi Mario, mi Cerezita . . .

CEREZITA: I'm still here, 'amá.

DOLORES (*staring at her daughter, momentarily confused*): Arturo, do you remember when I was big with Cere and the whole house was full of babies?

She exits, quietly muttering to herself. CEREZITA *presses her mouth to the raite button and goes over to the small open coffin.*

CEREZITA: Before the grown ones come to put you in the ground, they'll untie the ropes around your wrists and ankles. By then you are no longer in your body. The child's flesh hanging from that wood makes no difference to you. It is . . . you are a symbol. Nada más.

JUAN *appears at the window, taps it lightly.*

CEREZITA (*whispering*): Juan?

JUAN: Yes, it's me.

CEREZITA: Come in.

JUAN (*entering with a duffel bag*): Is everyone asleep?

CEREZITA: Yes.

Trying to contain his excitement, JUAN *gets down on his knees and starts pulling things out of the bag.*

CEREZITA: You hardly look like a gravedigger.

JUAN: Shovel. Flashlight. Rope. Did I forget anything?

CEREZITA: Do you know how beautiful you are?

JUAN: What?

CEREZITA: I've never seen you like this. You're almost glowing.

JUAN: I am?

CEREZITA: Glowing.

JUAN: Are the children waiting? (*He repacks the duffel bag.*)

CEREZITA: They'll meet us in front of the church. There's time yet.

JUAN: I saw Amparo today. She knows, Cere.

CEREZITA: She wouldn't stop us.

JUAN: No, but . . .

CEREZITA: What?

JUAN: She says it's dangerous. She says they'll shoot anything that moves out there in the field tonight.

CEREZITA: Then we'll have to leave the kids behind. I don't need them now. I have you. You're not afraid are you, Juan?

JUAN: No. Yes, I'm scared, but it's exciting.

CEREZITA: Things are gonna change now, Juan. You'll see.

JUAN (*walks over to the coffin, blesses it*): She looks peaceful.

CEREZITA: She is. What we do to her body won't disturb her peace.

JUAN: Yes, I'm supposed to know that.

CEREZITA: Nobody's dying should be invisible, Juan. Nobody's.

There is a pause. JUAN prays by the coffin. CEREZITA observes.

CEREZITA: Juan? . . .

JUAN: Hmm? . . .

CEREZITA: You know when they killed those priests in El Salvador?

JUAN: The Jesuits.

CEREZITA: Did you know they killed the housekeeper and her daughter, too?

JUAN: Yes.

CEREZITA: If the Jesuits died as priests, does that make them saints?

JUAN: I don't know. They're martyrs, heroes. They spoke out against the government.

CEREZITA: Did the housekeeper and her daughter?

JUAN: What?

CEREZITA: Speak out against the government?

JUAN: I don't think so.

CEREZITA: I don't either. It wasn't their job. I imagine they just changed the priests' beds, kept a pot of beans going, hung out the sábanas to dry. At least, the housekeeper did and the girl, she helped her mother. She did the tasks that young girls do . . . girls still living under the roof of their mother. And maybe sometimes one of the priests read to the girl, maybe . . . he taught her to read and she . . . fell in love with him, the teacher. (*Pause.*) Touch my hair, Juan.

Coming up from behind her, he touches her hair very tenderly, brings a strand to his face. He smells it, puts his hand to her cheek, caresses her. She moves her cheek deeper into the palm of his hand, moans softly. She lifts her face to his. He hesitates, then kisses her at first awkwardly, trying to find her mouth at the right angle. CEREZITA moans. Suddenly,

JUAN's face takes on a distanced look. He grabs CERE's cheeks between his hands.

CEREZITA: I want to taste you, Juan.

He hesitates, then kisses her again. CEREZITA's moaning increases, intensifies. He comes around behind her, presses his pelvis up against the backside of the raite. He brings her head against him, his fingers tangled in her hair.

CEREZITA: I want the ocean in my mouth.

She pulls at his shirt with her teeth, trying to bring him back around.

CEREZITA: Juan, help me. I need your hands.

JUAN *closes his eyes.*

CEREZITA: Juan, look at me.

He digs his pelvis into the raite, pulling her head deeper into him.

CEREZITA: Juan, where are you?

He pushes against her harder, deeper.

CEREZITA: Open your eyes. Juan.

He comes to orgasm.

CEREZITA: Juan.

He grabs the duffel bag and runs out.

CEREZITA: Juan!

After a few moments, the sound of an approaching helicopter, then gunshots are heard. Black out.

Scene Seven

Dawn. MARIO is lying on a park bench, wearing a jacket, the collar turned up, a knapsack at his feet. He has a constant cough. JUAN walks by. Still in his priest's clothes, he appears somewhat disheveled.

MARIO: Got a cigarette?

JUAN: Mario.

MARIO: Hello, Father.

JUAN: We'd almost given you up for lost.

MARIO: You're out pretty early.

JUAN: I . . . couldn't sleep.

MARIO: I've forgotten what sleep is.

JUAN: Why didn't you answer my messages?

MARIO: Wasn't even sure I was coming until I found myself hitching out on the interstate.

JUAN: You been to the house?

MARIO: Yes. Well . . . almost.

JUAN (*indicating the bench*): May I?

MARIO: For a cigarette.

JUAN: Oh, right.

> MARIO *gets up.* JUAN *sits beside him, lights up a cigarette for each of them.*

JUAN: You shouldn't be smoking, Mario . . . with that cough.

MARIO: Lung cancer's the least of my worries, Padre. (*They sit in silence for a few moments. Sounds of the highway can be heard in the distance.*) This place is strange. Just one hundred yards off that highway, and you're already right smack back into the heart of the Valley. In minutes, it feels like you never left, like it won't ever let you leave again, . . . like a Chicano Bunuel movie. (JUAN *smiles.*)

JUAN: Except it's too real.

MARIO: The city's no different. Raza's dying everywhere. Doesn't matter if it's crack or . . . pesticides, AIDS, it's all the same shit.

JUAN: Do you regret going, Mario?

MARIO: No. (*Pause.*) I've always loved sex, Father, always felt that whatever I had crippled or bent up inside me that somehow sex could cure it, that sex could straighten twisted limbs, like . . . the laying on of hands.

JUAN: Like tongues of fire.

MARIO: Yeah. Even holy like that . . . with the right person. (*Pause.*) And when you love your own sex, and they got your own hungry dark eyes staring back at you, well you're convinced that you could even cure death. And so you jus' keep kissing that same purple mouth, deeper and harder, and you keep whispering, "I'm gonna wipe all that sickness outta you, cousin." And then weeks and months and maybe even a year or two go by, and suddenly you realize you didn't cure nothing and that your family's dissolving right there inside of your hands.

JUAN (*pause*): And your blood family, Mario? . . .

MARIO: I've had to choose, Father. I can't come home. I'm not strong enough, I'm not a woman. I'm not suited for despair. I'm not suited to carry a burden greater than the weight of my own balls. (*He picks up his knapsack.*)

JUAN: You're leaving?

MARIO: I'm sick, Father. Tell my family in whatever way you can. (*He starts to exit.*)

JUAN: Mario.

He hands him the pack of cigarettes. MARIO *smiles and walks off. Fade out.*

Scene Eight

A few hours later. YOLANDA *wears a black slip and is ironing a black blouse.* CEREZITA *watches her.*

YOLANDA: My mom hasn't said one word to me about Lina. She just keeps asking what time mi 'apá's coming. What are we gonna do? We barely got a family left. (*She puts on the blouse, starts to button it.*)

CEREZITA: You gotta leave this place.

YOLANDA (*grabbing her breasts*): ¡Carajo! I can't stop them. I can't stop them from running.

CEREZITA: What?

YOLANDA: My breasts. They're so heavy, Cere. They're killing me. Nothing takes the pain away. They want a mouth and there's no mouth to relieve them. They feel like they're gonna burst open. I wish they would, I wish they would spill onto everything, turn everything to milk. Sweet milk. My baby's sweet mouth, I miss my baby. (*Her breasts run.*) Look at me. I'm a mess. They're dripping all over me. (*She grabs a bunch of tissues, continues stuffing them into her bra, taking them out and stuffing more in.*) Every time I think of her, they run. Nobody told my body my baby is dead. I still hear her crying and my breasts bleed fucking milk. I remember the smell of her skin and they bleed again. My body got used to being a mother, Cere. And then it's cut off . . . like that! A child's not supposed to die before her mother. It's not natural. It's not right. That's why you hear about women throwing themselves in front of speeding cars, blocking bullets to save their kid. I get it now. It's not about sacrifice. It's instinct. (*She pulls at her breasts.*) I want to rip them off of me. They feel like tombstones on my chest!

CEREZITA (*presses the button to her raite, crosses to* YOLANDA): Sister! I wish I had arms to hold you.

YOLANDA: Cere . . .

CEREZITA: It's almost over now, 'mana. You gotta get outta here, start a new family.

YOLANDA: I'm afraid, Cere. I think my womb is poisoned.

CEREZITA: No. Let me take the pain away. Your breasts, they're so heavy.

YOLANDA *goes to her, opens her blouse and brings* CERE's *face to her breast. The lights fade to black.*

Scene Nine

BONNIE *holds her doll in one hand and a large pair of scissors in the other.* CEREZITA *watches her as she begins to cut the doll's hair.*

BONNIE: This isn't going to hurt you, hija. It's for your own good.

CEREZITA: Bonnie, vente.

BONNIE *goes to her. They huddle together, speaking in whispers.*

CEREZITA (*aloud*): After this there will be no more sacrificial lambs. Not here in this valley. No more.

BONNIE *nods and exits as* JUAN *enters.* CEREZITA *will not look at him.*

JUAN: I came to see if you were all right. (*Pause.*) Cere, turn around. Please. . . . I heard there were gunshots. The children—

CEREZITA: The children were waiting for you. They were waiting for you with their little flashlights, their children's shovels, their children's hearts.

JUAN: I lost heart.

CEREZITA: Yes, you lost heart.

JUAN (*pause*): After I left here, I just started driving north. I didn't know where I was going, I was going nowhere. The fog was so thick. I could barely see the front end of the car. (*Pause.*) And it suddenly hit me, how this had happened once before, that I had done this before, somewhere else with some other—

CEREZITA: Pobre?

JUAN: Yes. (*Pause.*) I turned the car around.

CEREZITA: Why?

JUAN: I had to come back. See you.

CEREZITA: We had a plan, Juan, a plan of action. But your small fear stopped you.

JUAN: I couldn't after that. I—

CEREZITA: After what?

JUAN: It shouldn't have happened.

CEREZITA: Stop, Juan.

JUAN: I'm a priest, Cere. I'm not free. My body's not my own.

CEREZITA: It wasn't your body I wanted. It was mine. All I wanted was for you to make me feel like I had a body because, the fact is, I don't. I was denied one. But for a few minutes, a few minutes before you started *thinking*, I felt myself full of fine flesh filled to the bones in my toes. . . . I miss myself. Is that so hard to understand?

JUAN: No.

CEREZITA: And I'm sick of all this goddamn dying. If I had your arms and legs, if I had your dick for chrissake, you know what I'd do? I'd burn this motherless town down and all the poisoned fields around it. I'd give healthy babies to each and every childless woman who wanted one and I'd even stick around to watch those babies grow up! . . . You're a waste of a body.

JUAN: Cere . . .

BONNIE *reenters, carrying the small cross. The* CHILDREN *stand behind her.*

CEREZITA: I'm not gonna let you stop me, Juan. Nobody's going to stop me.

The lights fade to black.

Scene Ten

JUAN *has exited. In the half-darkness, the* CHILDREN *surround* CEREZITA *and begin to transform her as* BONNIE *cuts away at* CERE's *hair. Moments later, they scatter. The lights rise to reveal* DOLORES *standing in the doorway. A brilliant beam of light has entered the room and washes over* CEREZITA. *She is draped in the blue-starred veil of La Virgen de Guadalupe. Her head is tilted slightly toward the right, her eyes downcast in the Virgin's classic expression.* DOLORES *is riveted by the sight. The raite is covered in a white altar cross with the roses of Tepeyac imprinted upon it. The cross rests at the base of the raite. The light, brighter now, completely illuminates* CERE's *saintlike expression and the small cross.* DOLORES *drops to her knees.*

DOLORES: Mi virgen.

Black out.

Scene Eleven

The baby's coffin has been brought out, draped in a funeral cloth of white. DOLORES *stands by it, praying softly, then crosses to la virgen. She lifts up the veil slightly and touches* CEREZITA's *face.* DOLORES *exhibits a calm not previously witnessed in the play.*

DOLORES: And you usetu have such beautiful beautiful hair. But it was you, mi virgencita, that made this sacrificio para nosotros. (*Crossing herself with the rosary, she kneels before the image of la virgen.*) "El quinto misterio doloroso, la crucifixión." Querida virgen santísima, watch over nuestra baby Evalina.

She begins to pray the rosary. YOLANDA *enters, wearing a black chapel veil.*

YOLANDA: ¿Está lista, 'amá? . . . Cheezus! What's wrong with her? Why are you praying to her?

DOLORES: It was a sign from God.

YOLANDA: What sign? Cere-girl. Answer me!

DOLORES: Ya no 'stá.

YOLANDA: Whadayou mean, she's not there? Cere?

DOLORES: She went already to another place.

YOLANDA: What place?

DOLORES: A place inside herself. She said she was going on a long jornada. She tole me with her eyes.

YOLANDA: No, 'amá.

DOLORES: She gave me a sign, a sign of the cross. Esta mañana I found it, just like this. (*She takes the cross, holds it up to her.*) The sun was coming in por la ventana y la cruz estaba iluminada en luz. We've had no pertection, hija. La virgencita will protect us now.

YOLANDA: Cere. Talk to me.

DOLORES: ¡Imagínate! Un milagro un nuestra propia casa.

YOLANDA: 'Amá, what did you do to her?

DOLORES (*pause*): I pray, hija.

In the distance the sound of singing and the slow beat of a tambor.

EL PUEBLO (*singing*):

> 'Oh María, madre mía! Oh consuelo, del mortal!
> Amparadme y guiadme a la patria celestial!'

BONNIE *comes into the house and approaches* DOLORES.

DOLORES: ¿Qué quieres?

BONNIE: La cruz, Doña Lola. It's the funeral.

DOLORES (*as if realizing for the first time*): The funeral.

> DOLORES *reluctantly hands the cross over to her.* YOLANDA *goes to the coffin, hesitates for a brief moment, then tenderly lifts it up and carries it out to meet the procession, following* BONNIE. *Hearing the voices approaching,* DOLORES *pulls the curtain around* CEREZITA. *Outside,* ANA PEREZ *addresses the "camera."*

ANA PEREZ: This is Ana Pérez coming to you live from McLaughlin, California. Today is the funeral of Evalina Valle, the tenth child to die of cancer in this small Valley town.

> JUAN, *dressed in full vestments, accompanied by altar boys and* EL PUEBLO, *passes before the Valle house. They crane their necks to get a glimpse of* CEREZITA, *but* DOLORES *stands resolute before the window, shielding her from view.* YOLANDA *gives the altar boys the coffin. They all continue in procession,* BONNIE *leading with the cross.*

ANA PEREZ: Although funerals are becoming commonplace here in McLaughlin, rumors of a miracle occurrence in the family of the deceased have spread rapidly and have already attracted a huge following. Just before nine this morning, it was reported that Dolores Valle, the mother of Cerezita Valle, found a wooden cross in the disabled girl's sleeping chamber. The cross was illuminated in a wondrous glow and from that moment the young virgin has ceased to speak and has assumed an appearance and affect strikingly similar to the Virgin of Guadalupe . . . (*She spies* YOLANDA *as the procession passes.* This . . . virgin, this saint is your sister?

YOLANDA: I don't want to talk to you.

ANA PEREZ: The priest asked to be here.

YOLANDA: Father Juan?

ANA PEREZ: He said there was to be a crucifixion.

YOLANDA: My god! ¡Mi hija! (*She rushes off to catch up with the procession.*)

> EL PUEBLO *have arrived at the church steps.* JUAN *prays over the coffin, blessing it with holy water.* YOLANDA *hovers near the coffin.* DON GILBERTO *arrives with* AMPARO *in the wheelchair.* ANA PEREZ

stands on the sidelines, observing. The church bells toll.

JUAN: Señor, hazme un instrumento de tu paz. Donde hay odio . . .

EL PUEBLO: Que siembre yo amor;

JUAN: Donde hay injuria . . .

EL PUEBLO: Perdón;

JUAN: Donde hay duda . . .

EL PUEBLO: Fe;

JUAN: Donde hay deseperación . . .

EL PUEBLO: Esperanza;

> *They continue praying. In the Valle home,* DOLORES *has covered her head with a black rebozo. She starts to exit.*

CEREZITA: Let me go, 'amá.

DOLORES: Hija?

CEREZITA: I know about death. I know how to stop death.

DOLORES: ¿Has visto la cara de Dios?

CEREZITA: Sí, 'amá. I've seen the face of God. But I'm not free.

DOLORES: No entiendo.

CEREZITA: You tie my tongue, 'amá. How can I heal without my tongue? Do I have arms or legs?

DOLORES: I cut them from you.

CEREZITA: No 'amá. You gave birth to me. Eres mi madre.

DOLORES: Sí . . .

CEREZITA: Now, let . . . me . . . go.

> *Church bells resonate throughout the town. They call her to action. She turns back the curtain.* DOLORES *is stunned by the resolve in* CERE-ZITA's *eyes. There is no need for more words.* DOLORES *pushes the raite with la virgen out the door.*

JUAN: Pues es dando . . .

EL PUEBLO: Que recibimos;

JUAN: Es perdonando . . .

EL PUEBLO: Que somos perdonados;

JUAN: Y es muriendo . . .

EL PUEBLO: Que nacemos a la vida eter—

Upon the sight of la virgen, the prayer is interrupted. A hush falls over the crowd.

JUAN (*to himself*): My God, Cere, what have they done to you?

They arrive at the church steps. DOLORES *calls out to* ANA PEREZ.

DOLORES: Come, señorita. Come see how my baby se vuelve a santita. Come show the peepo.

ANA PEREZ *is noticeably shaken by the image of* CEREZITA. *She signals to the "cameraman" to begin filming. In procession,* EL PUEBLO *bring forth pictures of their dead and deformed children in offering to la virgen.*

EL PUEBLO (*singing*):

'Oh María, madre mía! Oh consuelo, del mortal!
Amparadme y guiadme a la patria celestial!'

The singing continues as they pin milagros to the white cloth of her raite. DOLORES *raises her hand to quiet the crowd.* CEREZITA's *eyes scan the faces of the people. There is a pause.*

CEREZITA: Put your hand inside my wound. Inside the valley of my wound, there is a people. A miracle people. In this pueblito where the valley people live, the river runs red with blood; but they are not afraid because they are used to the color red. It is the same color as the river that runs through their veins, the same color as the sun setting into the sierras, the same color of the pool of liquid they were born into. They remember this in order to understand why their fields, like the rags of the wounded, have soaked up the color and still bear no fruit. No lovely red fruit that el pueblo could point to and say yes, for this we bleed, for this our eyes go red with rage and sadness. They tell themselves red is as necessary as bread. They tell themselves this in a land where bread is a tortilla without maize, where the frijol cannot be cultivated. (*Pause.*) But we, we live in a land of plenty. The fruits that pass through your fingers are too many to count—luscious red in their strawberry wonder, the deep purple of the grape inviting, the tomatoes perfectly shaped and translucent. And yet, you suffer at the same hands. (*Pause.*) You are Guatemala, El Salvador. You are the Kuna y Tarahumara. You are the miracle people too, for like them the same blood runs through your veins. The same memory of a time when your deaths were cause for reverence and celebration, not shock and mourning. You are the miracle people because today, this day, that red memory will spill out from inside you and flood this valley con coraje. And you will be free. Free to name this land *Madre*. Madre Tierra. Madre Sagrada. Madre . . . Libertad. The radiant red mother . . . rising.

JUAN *moves to the center of the crowd to give a final bendición.* MARIO *appears upstage. He goes to* DOLORES. *They embrace.* EL PUEBLO *kneel as* JUAN *blesses them and all those witnessing the play.* BONNIE *approaches* JUAN *with the cross.*

BONNIE: Now is it time, Father?

JUAN *nods, then takes the cross from her. Another child brings* JUAN *some rope. He goes to* CEREZITA, *touches her cheek, and releases the locks on the raite. Her eyes do not leave him. He puts her mouthpiece attachment in place. They both turn to* YOLANDA. YOLANDA *now understands that she is to offer up her dead infant. She goes to the coffin, takes it from the altar boys, kisses it, then hands it over to* JUAN. CERE- ZITA *presses her mouth to the button of her raite and slowly turns toward the vineyard. The tambor begins to beat slowly, while* EL PUEBLO *watch in silence.* JUAN *and* CEREZITA *head out to the vineyard.* CEREZITA *pauses briefly as she passes her mother.*

CEREZITA: Mamá.

DOLORES *blesses her.* CEREZITA *and* JUAN *proceed offstage into the vineyards. Moments later, the shadow and sound of a helicopter pass overhead.* EL PUEBLO *watch the sky. Then there is the sudden sound of machine gun fire.* EL PUEBLO *let out a scream and drop to the ground, covering their heads in terror.* MARIO *suddenly rises, raises his fist into the air.*

MARIO: Burn the fields!

EL PUEBLO (*rising with him*): ¡Enciendan los files! (*They all, including* ANA PEREZ, *rush out to the vineyards, shouting as they exit.*) ¡Asesinos! ¡Asesinos! ¡Asesinos!

Moments later, there is the crackling of fire as a sharp red-orange glow spreads over the vineyard and the Valle home. The lights slowly fade to black.

End